LOUVRE

7 CENTURIES OF PAINTING

LOUVRE

7 CENTURIES OF PAINTING

Valérie Mettais

Preface by
PIERRE ROSENBERG
Member of the Académie française

PRESIDENT-DIRECTOR OF THE LOUVRE MUSEUM

art
lys

Cover : Jacques Louis David, The Corontion of Emperor Napoleon I and the Crowning
of Empress Josephine in the Notre-Dame cathedral in Paris,
2 December 1804, Paris, 1806-1807. Oil on canvas, 621 x 979 cm.

Page 2 : Victor Duval, The Grande Galerie of the Louvre,
paris, circa 1880. Oil on canvas, 65 x 70 cm.

Pages 6 and 7 : Hubert Robert, Development Project for thr Grande Galerie
of the Louvre in 1796, Paris, 1796. Oil on canvas, 46 x 55 cm.

Editorial co-ordination : Denis Kilian

Graphic design and layout : Martine Mène

editorial follow-up and picture reseach : Christian Ryo

Production : Pierre Kegels

One may wonder about the need for a new publication dedicated to the painting collections at the Louvre Museum, which is recognised as being one of the most beautiful and comprehensive in the world and, consequently, has been the subject of numerous guides, catalogues and other publications.

However, this book fulfils a rather distinctive role. It is not intended to be an exhaustive work, but simply attempts to help visitors find their way through the maze of European painting, from 13th-century Italian primitives to Delacroix and Ingres. It has therefore adopted an original format, which consists in arranging and commenting on the work around varied themes (these may include, for example, a particular country and period: French painters 1620-1650; an iconographical subject: the Crucifixion, the story of Saint John the Baptist; or simply an interpretation, or a particular school: the followers of Caravaggio in Italy, France and Holland etc.) while providing brief commentaries on some of the great masters whose work is well represented in the Louvre collections (Leonardo, Raphael and Poussin etc.).

This format has a particular advantage which takes away the monotony of a strictly chronological summary or an uninspired room-by-room description of the Painting Section. The reader's interest is therefore constantly renewed by a different approach, and the arrangements between the commentaries and the themes provide the bases for a genuine understanding of the history of painting - and, I sincerely hope, the desire to develop this knowledge by visiting the Louvre again and again.

PIERRE ROSENBERG
Member of the Académie française
PRESIDENT-DIRECTOR OF THE LOUVRE MUSEUM

CONTENTS

13th - 14th CENTURY

THE DUECENTO

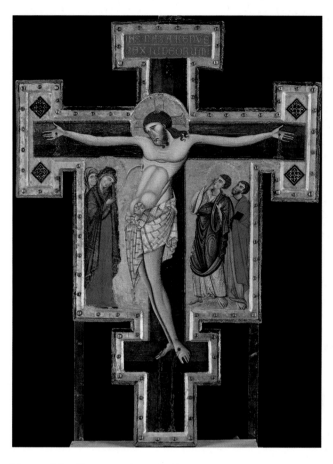

Master of San Francesco, *Crucifix*, Umbria,
circa 1265-1270. Tempera on wood, 96.5 x 73 cm.

Italian painter, *Saint Francis of Assisi*,
Latium, mid-13th century.
Tempera on wood, 95.4 x 38.7 cm.

Teaching, enlightening, edifying, stirring emotion or instilling fear… Such was the role of Christian images, according to Saint Bonaventure, a Franciscan of Tuscany, at the end of the *Duecento*, circa 1260: "They have been invented due to the lack of education of the common people who are unable to read the Scriptures, but may thus, through this genre of sculptures and paintings instead of books, discover more plainly the mysteries of our faith. Likewise, they have been introduced owing to the lack of fervour, so that people who remain unmoved to religious devotion by Christ's actions in our favour, with which we constantly fill their ears, may at least be prompted to faith when with the eyes of the body they behold them as present so to speak" *(Book of Sentences)*.

Guido da Siena, *The Nativity*, Siena, circa 1275-1280.
Tempera on wood, 36.4 x 47.5 cm.

Guido da Siena, *The Presentation in the Temple*, Siena, circa 1275-1280.
Tempera on wood, 34.5 x 48.5 cm.

CIMABUE, GIOTTO

The Middle Ages was a period full of colour, and blues, reds and yellows experienced a real revival both in Northern Europe and in Italy. In the 13th century, Cimabue then Giotto used artificial and vegetable pigments which intensify the deep, strong hues. Ultramarine, often used to drape the enthroned Virgin in a cloak of glory, is extracted from azurite or lapis lazuli, a stone originating in the Indies and available in Venice, Genoa and Pisa. The range of reds includes carmine made from cochineal, and sulphur and mercury vermilion, appearing here and there in a predella. The yellow is obtained from tin, lead or orpiment (arsenic trisulphide), and haloes of gold leaf, enhanced with green or sometimes red, encircle the faces of the angels.

Cenni di Peppi, known as Cimabue,
The Enthroned Virgin and Child Enthroned Surrounded by Six Angels, Pisa, circa 1270. Tempera on wood, 427 x 280 cm.

Giotto di Bondone, *Saint Francis of Assisi Receiving the Stigmata*, predella: *The Vision of Pope Innocent III, The Pope Approving the Statutes of the Order* and *Saint Francis Preaching to the Birds*, Pisa, circa 1295-1300. Tempera on wood, 313 x 163 cm.

"IT WAS
THE THIRD HOUR
WHEN THEY CRUCIFIED HIM"

Depicting the Crucifixion which took place on the mount of Golgotha in the presence of a few well-known figures and Roman soldiers: such was the iconographical theme imposed on artists, a theme taken from the New Testament: "And they brought Jesus to the place called Golgotha (which means the place of a skull). And they offered him wine mingled with myrrh, but he did not take it. And they crucified him, and divided his garments among them, casting lots for them, to decide what each should take. And it was the third hour, when they crucified him. And the inscription of the charge against him read, "The King of the Jews." And with him they crucified two robbers, one on his right and one on his left." (Gospel of Mark 15, 22-26).

△ Above right:
Jean de Beaumetz,
*Calvary with
Carthusian Monk*,
Carthusian Monastery
of Champmol, near Dijon,
1389-1395.
Tempera on wood,
60 x 48.5 cm.

△ Above left:
Studio of Giotto di
Bondone, *Crucifix*,
Florence, 15th century.
Tempera on wood,
277 x 225 cm.

◁ Master of 1333,
*The Crowning
of the Virgin,
The Crucifixion*, 1333.
Tempera on wood,
135 x 73 cm.

◁ Follower of Giotto di Bondone,
The Crucifixion, Naples, circa 1330.
Oil on wood, 89.3 x 59 cm.

◁ Left:
Italian painter,
*The Unbelief
of Saint Thomas*,
Padua (?), first half
of the 14th century.
Tempera on wood,
28.7 x 20.4 cm.

◁ Right:
Master of the Codex
of Saint George,
*The Enthroned
Virgin and Child
Surrounded by Angels,
Saint John the Baptist,
Saint Peter and
Two Saints*, Tuscany,
circa 1315-1330.
Tempera on wood,
56 x 21 cm.

△ Master of Monteoliveto, *The Enthroned Virgin and Child Surrounded by a Female Saint, Saint Paul, Saint Peter and Saint Dominic*, first half of the 14th century. Tempera on wood, 39 x 26.5 cm.

△ Pietro Lorenzetti, *The Adoration of the Magi*, Siena, circa 1335-1340. Tempera on wood, 30 x 20.5 cm.

△ Studio of Bernardo Daddi, *The Nativity and the Proclamation to the Shepherds*, detail of the left panel of *The Virgin and Child Surrounded by Angels and Saints* (see p. 17), Florence, first half of the 14th century. Tempera on wood.

FRENCH MONARCHS

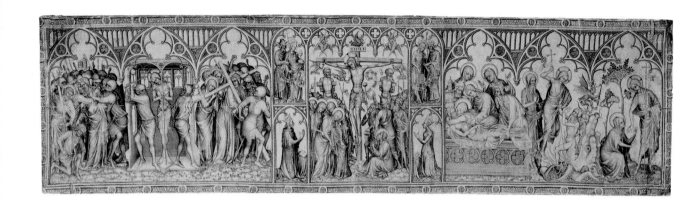

By associating their image with scenes of the Passion, the monarchs bore witness to their piety in the eyes of the subjects of the French Kingdom, and linked their earthly power with celestial omnipotence: Charles V *Le Sage* and Jeanne de Bourbon, kneeling, pray on either side of a Crucifixion.

Of Jean II *Le Bon*, held captive in England from 1356 until his death in 1363, there remains a profile outlined in ochre on a gold background, a precious royal image, the first autonomous portrait known to date, and the first easel painting.

Painter working in Paris,
The Frontal of Narbonne, circa 1375-1380.
Black ink on silk, 77.5 x 286 cm.

Right page:
Painter working in Paris,
Jean II Le Bon, King of France (1350-1364),
circa 1355. Tempera on wood, 59.8 x 44.6 cm.

23

15th CENTURY

THE DUKES OF BURGUNDY

By establishing Dijon as a political capital, Duke Philippe II *Le Hardi* transformed Burgundy at the end of the 14th century into a major cultural centre. Later, his son Jean *sans Peur* surrounded himself with numerous Flemish and Parisian painters, sculptors and architects, such as Jean de Beaumetz, Jean Malouel and Henri Bellechose. However, when Philippe III *Le Bon* chose to settle in Flanders in 1419, the whole thing collapsed, and everyone - the Court and the artists - was forced to leave. Bellechose, who remained in Dijon, died in poverty in about 1440. Now penniless and "provincial", Burgundy had no use for painters.

French painter, *Jean sans Peur, Duke of Burgundy (1404-1419)*, antique copy after a lost original dating from the 15th century. Oil on wood, 29 x 21 cm.

Jean Malouel, *Pietà*, known as the *Large Round Pietà*, Dijon, circa 1400. Tempera on wood, d: 64.5 cm.

Painter working in Paris or Burgundy, *The Entombment*, circa 1400. Tempera on wood, 32.8 x 21.3 cm.

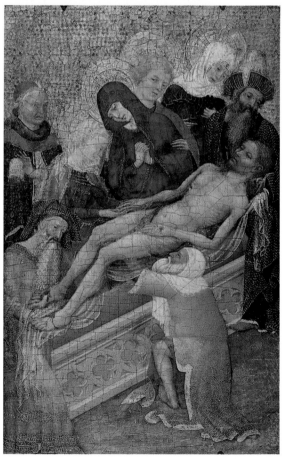

Henri Bellechose, *Saint Denis Altarpiece*, Dijon, 1416. Tempera on wood transposed onto canvas, 162 x 211 cm.

THE BODY
EXPOSED
TO SUFFERING

"To imitate Christ" is to desire to imitate his suffering, to suffer in his image. In 1441, a book on spiritual devotion appeared, destined to become immensely popular in the Christian world: *Imitation of Christ*, written by Canon Thomas à Kempis. The devotional altarpieces of the 15th century bear the mark of this piety which upholds pain and death: with painstaking detail, the painters emphasise the cruelty of torturers or the martyrdom of the dying.

△ Painter working in Paris, *The Pity of Our Lord*, known as the *Small Round Pietà*, Paris, pre-1410. Tempera on wood, d: 23 cm.

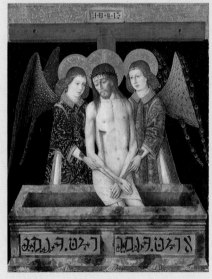

△ Spanish painter, *The Dead Christ Between Two Angels*, Valencia, end of the 15th century. Oil on wood, 63 x 50 cm.

△ Top: Cosmè Tura, *Pietà*, Ferrara, circa 1480. Oil on wood, 132 x 268 cm.

△ Master LCz, *The Scourging of Christ*, Bamberg, circa 1490-1500. Oil on wood, 78 x 60.8 cm.

△Jaime Huguet,
The Scourging of Christ,
Barcelona, 1450-1460.
Oil on wood, 92 x 156 cm.

◁Left: Bernardo Martorell,
Saint George Tortured by Dragging,
Barcelona, circa 1435.
Oil on wood, 107 x 53 cm.

◁Right: Bernardo Martorell,
The Scourging of Saint George,
Barcelona, circa 1435.
Oil on wood, 107 x 53 cm.

VAN EYCK, VAN DER WEYDEN, PETRUS CHRISTUS

Left:
Jan van Eyck, *Chancellor Rolin's Virgin*, known as *The Virgin of Autun*, Bruges, circa 1435.
Oil on wood, 66 x 62 cm.

Below:
Rogier van der Weyden, *The Annunciation*, Brussels, circa 1435.
Oil on wood, 86 x 93 cm.

According to Carel van Mander in his portrayal in 1604 of the van Eyck brothers, two painters from Bruges who perfected the technique of oil painting, Italy has something to learn from Flanders: "Thus abandoning egg tempera coated with varnish, [Jan] in his searching aimed to produce a coating that would not need to dry in the open air and would, above all, spare painters the necessity of resorting to the action of sunlight. He tried a succession of oils and other substances, and found that linseed oil and walnut oil had particularly good drying properties. [...] after several attempts, he discovered that pigments thinned with oil combined perfectly, were waterproof and, lastly, that oil gave a more brilliant sheen without the aid of varnish." This formula was used in Bruges by Petrus Christus and in Brussels by van der Weyden, and began to spread throughout Europe.

Rogier van der Weyden,
Braque Family Triptych:
Christ Between the Virgin
and Saint John the Evangelist (central panel),
Saint John the Baptist (left panel)
and *Saint Mary Magdalene* (right panel),
Brussels, circa 1450. Oil on wood,
41 x 68 cm (central panel),
41 x 34 cm (side panels).

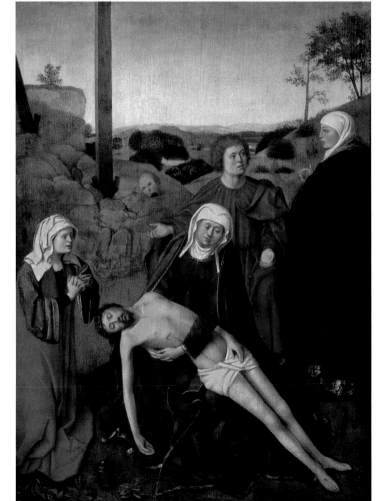

Petrus Christus,
The Lamentation of Christ,
Bruges, circa 1435-1440.
Oil on wood, 38 x 30.4 cm.

MUSICIANS, WORSHIPPERS AND AVENGING MESSENGERS

They create the music of the heavenly realms and play every kind of instrument. Often adorned with wings and halos, they are divine messengers sent down to Earth. Warriors clothed in armour, they slay dragons and demons, and weigh souls during the Last Judgement. Full of symbolism and history, angels also serve as a stylistic exercise since the painter is required, on each occasion, to establish an appearance, allocate a colour and determine a place.

△ Top left: Biagio d'Antonio, *The Virgin and Child Surrounded by Six Angels and the Young Saint John the Baptist*, Florence, end of the 15th century. Oil(?) on wood, 48 x 35 cm.

▷ Left: Stefano di Giovanni, known as Sassetta, *The Virgin and Child Surrounded by Six Angels*, central panel of the triptych, Borgo San Sepolcro, 1437-1444. Tempera on wood, 207 x 118 cm.

△ Studio of Guido di Pietro, known as Fra Angelico, *Angel in Adoration*, Florence, 15th century. Tempera on wood, 37 x 23 cm

△ Top: Francesco Marmitta, *The Virgin and Child Surrounded by Saint Benedict, Saint Quentin, and Two Angels* (detail), Parma, end of the 15th century. Oil on wood.

△ Above:
Sano di Pietro,
*Saint Jerome
Dreams That
He Is Scourged
by Two Angels
on the Orders
of Christ*, Siena,
1444. Tempera
on wood,
23.5 x 35.5 cm.

△ Top left:
Michel Sittow,
*The Crowning
of the Virgin*, Toro,
circa 1496-1504.
Oil on wood,
24.5 x 18.3 cm.

△ Top centre:
Painter from Amiens
or Burgundy,
*The Mass
for Saint Gregory*,
Carthusian
Monastery of
Champmol,
near Dijon,
circa 1450.
Oil on wood,
60 x 39.5 cm.

△ Centre:
Lorenzo di Credi,
The Annunciation,
Pistoia, 1478-1485.
Oil on wood,
16 x 60 cm.

△ Raffaello Sanzio,
known as Raphael, *Angel*,
fragment of the Saint Nicholas
of Tolentino altarpiece, 1500-1501.
Oil on wood, 58 x 36 cm.

△ Bartholomaüs Zeitblom,
The Annunciation, central part
of the altarpiece, Ulm, circa 1490.
Oil on wood, 62.5 x 88.5 cm.

△ Ercole de' Roberti,
Saint Michael, décor
of a pilaster framing
an altarpiece, Bologna,
circa 1473. Oil on wood,
26.5 x 11 cm.

Guido di Pietro, known as Fra Angelico,
Christ Bestowing a Blessing,
Florence, mid-15th century.
Tempera on wood, d: 12 cm.

Occasionally signed in the presence of a lawyer, contracts governed the relationship between the painter and his client when a
painting was commissioned. The contract would include the
obligations of each party together with the different formalities:
the choice of subject - the artist would agree to honour the composition chosen in the preliminary drawing, the delivery date, the
price of the work, which would depend upon the rarity of the
materials used, the number of assistants, and time spent... Some
sponsors would even pay per square foot for a fresco, while
others would pay a higher price for pigments and gold which
were visible on the support. If the painter was called Fra Angelico
the Dominican of Fiesole, it would be left up to him to determine the price of an altarpiece, since it would seem rather inap-
propriate to negotiate with a Dominican friar.

Top right: Guido di Pietro, known as Fra Angelico,
The Crowning of the Virgin,
predella: *Seven Scenes from the Life of Saint Dominic*,
Fiesole, circa 1434-1435. Tempera on wood, 209 x 206 cm.

Right page: Three scenes from the predella:
*The Dream of Innocent III, Saint Peter and Saint Paul
Appearing to Saint Dominic,* and *The Death of Saint Dominic.*

Right: Guido di Pietro, known as Fra Angelico,
The Martyrdom of Saint Cosmas and Saint Damian,
Florence, circa 1440. Tempera on wood, 37.3 x 46.1 cm.

Paolo Uccello,
*The Battle
of San Romano:
The Counter-attack
of Micheletto
da Cotignola*,
Florence,
circa 1450-1456.
Tempera on wood,
187 x 317 cm.

According to a tradition which goes back to the *Quattrocento*, the architect Filippo Brunelleschi is believed to have invented "artificial perspective" in Florence in the 1430s. Concerning both the art and science of representation, this discovery would henceforth be a matter for all, mathematicians, theoreticians and, of course, painters. Paolo Uccello thus strives to give the illusion of three dimensions in his two-dimensional painting; he intersperses vanishing lines which converge towards a central point, alternates close and distant objects, and composes and contrasts the foreground and background.

Italian painter, *Five Masters of the Florentine Renaissance: Giotto, Uccello, Donatello, Manetti, Brunelleschi*, Florence, 16th century. Oil on wood, 65.5 x 21.3 cm.

GEOMETRICAL PERSPECTIVE: CREATING A SPACE

Staircases, paving and pilasters are so many devices which heighten the depth of a painting. According to the mathematician Antonio Manetti in about 1475, it is all a matter of perspective: "what painters today call perspective is that part of the science of perspective which practically amounts to reducing or enlarging discerningly and systematically [...] objects which are respectively distant or close by - whether houses, plains, mountains or landscapes".

△ Paolo Uccello,
The Battle of San Romano
(detail, see p. 36), Florence, circa
1450-1456.
Tempera on wood.

△ Nicolas Dipre, *Presentation of the Virgin in the Temple*, panel of a predella, Avignon, circa 1498. Tempera on wood, 33 x 51 cm.

△ Top: Andrea Mantegna,
Calvary, Mantua, 1457-1460.
Oil on wood, 76 x 96 cm.

△Master of the View of Sainte Gudule, *Saint Géry Preaching*(?), known as *Pastoral Instruction*, Brussels, circa 1475-1480. Oil on wood, 98 x 69 cm.

△Top: Filippino Lippi, *Esther Faints Before Ahasuerus*, Florence, circa 1475. Oil on wood, 48 x 132 cm.

△Carlo Braccesco, *The Annunciation*, central panel of the triptych, Genoa, circa 1480-1500. Oil on wood, 158 x 107 cm.

JEAN FOUQUET, JEAN HEY

In their portraits of sovereigns, persons of distinction and children in their scenes of piety, French painters such as Jean Fouquet and Jean Hey employ a repertoire of poses, gestures, and motifs familiar to onlookers of their time. Combined with facial expressions, the position of the hands served to set the scene of a painting: pressing one's hands to one's chest signifies emotion; an outstretched hand is a presentation, or sometimes an invitation; turning the palm of one's hand outwards is reserved for the pious; covering one's face with one's hands refers to shame, and putting one's hands together is a sign of prayer… The details and objects - a bunch of keys or a perfume vessel - tell the story of a figure.

Jean Fouquet, *Charles VII, King of France (1422-1461)*, Tours, circa 1445. Oil on wood, 85.7 x 70.6 cm.

Jean Fouquet, *Guillaume Jouvenel des Ursins*, Tours, circa 1460. Oil on wood, 93 x 73.2 cm.

Jean Fouquet, *Self-portrait*, Tours, circa 1450. Enamelled copper, d: 6.8 cm.

Jean Hey,
known as The Master of Moulins,
Pierre II, Lord of Beaujeu,
Duke of Bourbon,
Presented by Saint Peter,
Bourbonnais, circa 1492-1493.
Oil on wood, 73 x 65 cm.

Jean Hey,
known as The Master of Moulins,
Suzanne of Bourbon,
or *Praying Child*, Bourbonnais,
circa 1492-1493.
Oil on wood, 27 x 16.5 cm.

Jean Hey,
known as The Master of Moulins,
Presumed Portrait
of Madeleine of Burgundy,
Lady of Laage, Presented
by Saint Mary Magdalene,
Bourbonnais, circa 1490-1493.
Oil on wood, 56 x 40 cm.

PROVENCE

French painter, *Boulbon Altarpiece (The Suffering Christ, Saint Agricol and a Giver)*, Provence, circa 1460. Tempera on wood transposed onto canvas, 172 x 227 cm.

The theory of proportions must not be ignored by artists. This theory is taught in *The Book of Art* by Cennino Cennini of Florence, which thus reflects the figurative canons in force at the beginning of the 15ᵗʰ century, rules which may also be perceived in the *Pietà* and *The Suffering Christ* from the Provençal studios: "the first measurement that you would need to adopt in order to draw must be one of the three parts of the face, which is divided into three sections in all, that is, the forehead, the eyes and nose, and lastly the chin and mouth. If you adopt one of these, it will be your guide for the whole figure". He then goes on to the anatomical details: "A man's body corresponds to the length of his arms in the form of a cross. His arms and hands extended reach the middle of the thigh. [...] He has one rib less than women, on the left side. There are bones in every part of a man's body."

Nicolas Dipre, *The Nativity of the Virgin*, panel of a predella, Avignon, circa 1498. Tempera on wood, 29.7 x 50.8 cm.

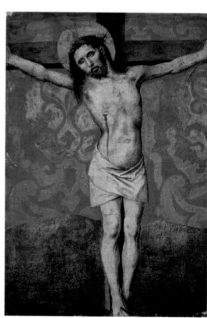

Barthélemy d'Eyck, *The Crucified Christ*, Aix-en-Provence, circa 1450. Tempera on wood, 25 x 17.5 cm.

Enguerrand Quarton, *Pietà of Villeneuve-lès-Avignon*, Avignon, circa 1455. Tempera on wood, 163 x 218 cm.

PARIS

The background of a painting sometimes reveals contemporary landscapes or depicts the structure of a town and its monuments. Such was the history of the altarpiece commissioned by the Paris Parliament to adorn the great chamber during the reign of Charles VII. On the left, behind Saint Louis dressed in a cloak decorated with fleur-de-lis, is the *Tour de Nesle* of the Philippe Auguste wall – this would be destroyed in the 17th century and replaced by the Mazarine library; the Louvre is shown stretching along the banks of the Seine, and one can also see the *Hôtel du Petit-Bourbon* – which has now disappeared. On the right, behind the decapitated Saint Denis and Charlemagne, standing on the *Ile de la Cité* is the palace which was the then seat of Parliament.

Master of Coëtivy, *Donor and Apostles*, fragment of *The Raising of Lazarus*, Paris, circa 1455-1460. Oil on wood, 78.5 x 35 cm.

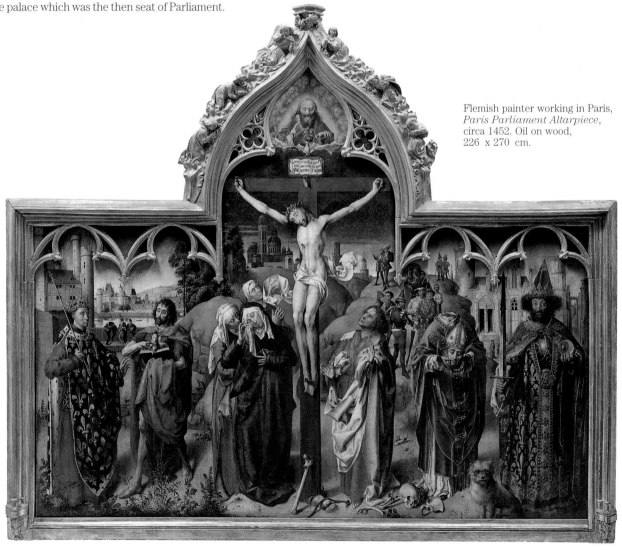

Flemish painter working in Paris, *Paris Parliament Altarpiece*, circa 1452. Oil on wood, 226 x 270 cm.

GÉRARD DE SAINT-JEAN, DIRK BOUTS

Geertgen tot Sint Jans, known as Gérard de Saint-Jean,
The Raising of Lazarus, Haarlem, circa 1480.
Oil on wood, 127 x 97 cm.

Dirk Bouts, the Elder, *The Lamentation of Christ*,
Louvain, circa 1460. Oil on wood, 69 x 49 cm.

Each minor detail attracts the eye, ultimately requiring contemplation
of the whole piece. By depicting scenes of the life and death of Christ,
striving for extreme realism, the Flemish painters joined with and encouraged religious practice. They achieve anatomical and physical precision: a thin, stretched out body, blood from the wound running along
the thigh to the inside of the knee. They achieve decorative precision,
down to the rendering of the materials: a man clothed in striped robes
holds his nose, recoiling from the odour of the resurrected corpse. They
achieve pathetic precision: a tear on the cheek and drops of blood on the
forehead of a man of pain.

Studio of Dirk Bouts, the Elder, *The Suffering Christ*, Louvain, 15th century. Oil on wood, 38.6 x 29.4 cm.

MEMLING

Originating from the Rhine region, in 1465 Hans Memling achieved "the right of bourgeoisie" in Bruges, the Flemish city governed by the House of Burgundy. Overwhelmed by commissions from bankers, merchants and aldermen, the painter gained high recognition and a substantial fortune - his legacy thus included three residences. Bruges was then home to thirty-five thousand souls. Making its living predominantly from the woollen cloth trade, the city was the leading financial market in northern Europe.

Hans Memling,
Angel Holding an Olive Branch,
fragment of an altarpiece, Bruges, circa 1480.
Oil on wood, 16.4 x 11 cm.

Hans Memling,
Portrait of an Old Woman,
Bruges, circa 1470-1475.
Oil on wood, 35 x 29 cm.

Hans Memling,
Triptych of the Resurrection
(central panel),
*The Martyrdom
of Saint Sebastian* (left panel)
and *The Ascension* (right panel),
Bruges, circa 1490.
Oil on wood,
61 x 44 cm (central panel),
61.7 x 18 cm (side panels).

Hans Memling,
*The Virgin and Child
Flanked by Saint James
and Saint Dominic
Presenting the Donors
and Their Family*,
known as
Jacques Floreins' Virgin,
Bruges, circa 1485.
Oil on wood, 130 x 160 cm.

PRINCES, WARRIORS, GENTLEMEN AND ARTISTS

In certain respects, portraits prolong the life of the deceased. This is achieved by painting, writes Leone Battista Alberti: "Painting has a completely divine force which makes it possible not only to restore to life those who are absent, as we say out of friendship, but also after several centuries to reveal the dead to the living, making them recognisable for the utmost pleasure of the beholder in the greatest admiration for the artist. Plutarch tells that Cassandra, one of Alexander's generals, started to tremble before an image in which he recognised Alexander who was already dead and in it perceived the majesty of the King; and that Agesilaus the Lacedaemonian, knowing he was very ugly, refused to leave his image to posterity and, for this very reason, never allowed his portrait to be painted" (*On Painting*, 1434).

△ Luca Signorelli and studio, *Group of Figures Standing*, Cortona, circa 1490-1500. Oil on wood, 109 x 72.5 cm.

◁ Albrecht Dürer, *Portrait of the Artist Holding a Thistle*, Nuremberg, 1493. Oil on parchment pasted onto canvas, 56.5 x 44.5 cm.

△ Piero della Francesca, *Portrait of Sigismond Malatesta*, Rimini, circa 1451. Oil on wood, 44 x 34 cm.

△ Top: Antonio Pisano, known as Pisanello, *Portrait of Princess d'Este*, Verona, circa 1436-1438. Oil on wood, 43 x 30 cm.

◁ Left:
French painter,
Man Holding a Glass of Wine,
circa 1460. Oil on wood,
63 x 44 cm.

◁ Centre:
Ludger Tom Ring, the Younger,
Portrait of a Woman,
known as *The Delphic Sybil*,
Münster, end of the 15th century.
Oil on wood, 44 x 31 cm.

◁ Right:
Sandro Botticelli,
Portrait of a Man,
Florence, end of the 15th century.
Oil on wood, 57 x 39.8 cm.

◁ Painter from Provence,
Three Prophets, Arles,
second half of the 15th century.
Oil on wood, 61 x 94.5 cm.

△ Antonello da Messina, *Portrait of a Man*, known as *The Condottiere*, Venice, 1475. Oil on wood, 36.2 x 30 cm.

△ Marco Marziale, *Portrait of a Man*, Venice, between 1493 and 1507. Oil on wood, 36 x 25 cm.

△ Domenico Ghirlandaio, *Portrait of an Old Man and Young Boy*, Florence, circa 1488. Tempera on wood, 63 x 46 cm.

COLOGNE ALTARPIECES

Because artists in the 15th century were primarily considered to be artisans, producers of images paid by a prince or placed in the service of God, few signatures appear on the paintings. The Cologne School, then situated in the largest city of Germany, honours this tradition: no names are visible on the altarpieces; the painters are referred to as "masters" since their identity is unknown. Thus, some artists would use subtle, indirect means in order to show their merit or attribute a piece to themselves: blend a self-portrait in with a crowd of figures, discreetly sketch their image on the frame of the painting, appear in *trompe-l'œil* or distorted in a mirror.

Master of the Holy Family,
Altarpiece of the Seven Joys of Mary,
Cologne, circa 1480.
Oil on wood, 127 x 182 cm.

Master of Saint-Séverin,
The Circumcision,
Cologne, circa 1490.
Oil on wood, 90 x 75 cm.

Master of Saint Bartholomew,
The Descent from the Cross,
Cologne, commissioned by the Abbaye
Saint-Antoine (?) in Paris,
circa 1500-1505. Oil on wood,
227 x 210 cm.

Master of the Saint Ursula Legend,
*In the Court of Her Father
Saint Ursula Announces
Her Decision to Go on a Pilgrimage
to Rome with Eleven Thousand
Virgins*, Cologne, end of the 15th
century. Oil on wood, 129 x 155 cm.

THE STUDIOLO OF URBINO

The Duke and Condottiere Federico da Montefeltro devoted a room of his Urbino palace to reflection and contemplation. The *studiolo*, or study, was the place where this man of power and soldier proved himself a humanist smitten with ancient, Christian and contemporary culture. He commissioned two artists hailing from different backgrounds - Joos van Wassenhove was Flemish and Berruguete, Spanish - to decorate his walls: twenty-eight portraits of distinguished figures evoke a few areas of learning: theology with the Church Fathers, from Saint Jerome to Saint Thomas Aquinas; Greek philosophy and astronomy with Aristotle, Plato and Ptolemy; and Latin tragedy and poetry with Seneca and Virgil…

Joos van Wassenhove and Pedro Berruguete, *Aristotle* (top), *Plato* (left) and *Ptolemy* (right), Urbino, circa 1476. Oil on wood, 104 x 68 cm, 101.4 x 69 cm and 98 x 66.3 cm.

Joos van Wassenhove and Pedro Berruguete, *Saint Thomas Aquinas*, Urbino, circa 1476. Oil on wood, 114 x 76 cm.

Joos van Wassenhove and Pedro Berruguete, *Saint Jerome*, Urbino, circa 1476. Oil on wood, 116.7 x 68.6 cm.

PAINTING CAN
ALSO WORK
MIRACLES

Many roles are assigned to religious scenes: they must reveal that which is hidden, depict the supernatural and the ineffable, and portray apparitions and visions. The miracle of painting resides in the creation of the invisible.

▷ Guido di Pietro, known as Fra Angelico, *The Dispute of Saint Dominic and The Miracle of the Book*, part of the predella *The Crowning of the Virgin* (cf. p. 34), Fiesole, circa 1430-1435. Tempera on wood.

▷ Stefano di Giovanni, known as Sassetta, *The Blessed Ranieri Rasini Sets the Poor Free from a Florence Prison*, panel of a predella, Borgo San Sepolcro, circa 1437-1444. Tempera on wood, 43.4 x 63.3 cm.

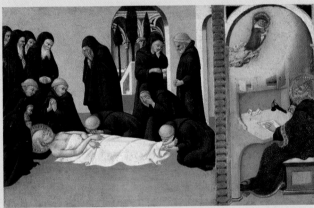

△ Top and above:
Sano di Pietro,
*Saint Jerome Appearing
in the Heavens to Sulpice
Sévère Then, by the Side
of Saint John the Baptist,
to Saint Augustine* and
*The Death of Saint
Jerome in the Presence
of His Disciples and
The Vision of Bishop
Saint Cyril of Jerusalem*,
Siena, 1444. Tempera on
wood, 23.5 x 37 cm.

▷ Luca Signorelli
(attributed to),
Saint Jerome in Ecstasy,
Cortona, circa 1505.
Oil on canvas, 69 x 49 cm.

△ Flemish Disciple
of Simon Marmion,
*The Miracle
of the True Cross*,
circa 1480.
Oil on wood,
68.2 x 58.7 cm.

◁ Disciple
of Stephan Lochner,
*The Miracle
of Saint Voult*,
Cologne,
mid-15th century.
Oil on wood,
20.3 x 12.7 cm.

MANTEGNA

Andrea Mantegna, *Mars and Venus*, known as *Parnassus*, Ducal Palace of Mantua, Studiolo of Isabelle d'Este, pre-1497. Tempera on canvas, 159 x 192 cm.

For an artist in the 15th century, being in the service of a powerful dynasty was the guarantee of total security and recognition. For forty-six years, from 1460 to his death in 1506, Andrea Mantegna was paid a wage by the Gonzaga family who reigned over Mantua: his monthly salary amounted to fifteen ducats, comfortable lodgings awaited him and his family, and wheat and firewood were provided. Although Mantegna was essentially a painter, adorning the palace with mythological compositions, he was also an adviser, chaperon and courtier, and was required to fulfil the requests of his employer, such as that expressed by Lodovico Gonzaga in 1469: "I would like you to do two drawings from life of two turkeys, one male and one female, and have them sent here to me, because I would like to have them woven by my tapestry-makers: you will be able to study the turkeys in the garden of Mantua."

Andrea Mantegna, *Minerva Driving Away Vice from the Garden of Virtue*, Ducal Palace of Mantua, Studiolo of Isabelle d'Este, 1497-1502. Tempera on canvas, 160 x 192 cm.

Andrea Mantegna, *Saint Sebastian*, Mantua, circa 1480. Tempera on canvas, 255 x 140 cm.

◁Left:
Piero di Cosimo,
*The Virgin and Child
with a Dove*,
Florence, circa 1485-1490.
Oil on wood,
87 x 58 cm.

◁Right:
Dirk Bouts, the Elder,
*The Virgin Seated
with the Child*,
Louvain, circa 1470.
Oil on wood,
20 x 12 cm.

◁Left:
Andrea Mantegna,
*The Virgin and Child
Surrounded
by Six Saints
and Adored by Gian-
Francesco II Gonzaga*,
known as *The Virgin
of Victory* (detail),
Mantua, 1495-1496.
Oil on canvas,
285 x 168 cm.

◁Right:
Studio of Dirk Bouts,
the Elder,
The Virgin of Pain,
Louvain, circa 1450.
Oil on wood,
38.6 x 29.7 cm.

BOTTICELLI

Sandro Botticelli, *Venus and the Graces Offering Gifts to a Young Girl*,
Florence, circa 1480-1483. Fresco, 211 x 283 cm.

Sandro Botticelli, *Young Man before the Assembly of the Liberal Arts*,
Florence, circa 1480-1483. Fresco, 237 x 269 cm.

The Percier and Fontaine Room,
on the first floor of the Denon Wing.

"Sandro Botticelli paints excellently both on panels and on walls. His work has a virile air and is executed according to the best method": thus speaks the messenger of the Duke of Milan, judging the qualities of the great Florentine artists in 1490. What exactly is this "virile air" attributed to the work of Botticelli? And what is "the best method"? These considerations today seem obscure since we have lost the meaning of 15th-century expression. As for identifying the liberal arts at the centre of a fresco, one must also be aware that there were seven in total and that they were taught at the University: arithmetic, astronomy, geometry and music formed the *quadrivium*, while grammar, rhetoric and dialectic formed the *trivium*.

VENICE

A meeting point of different influences and a Mecca of business, Venice was a thriving city. Governed by merchants and bankers, it was open to the world, traded with the East and the northern countries, established trading posts as far away as China, took an interest in humanism and developed printing - at the beginning of the following century, Venice would become the major European centre for books. It also nurtured a school of painting, to which belonged the Bellini and Carpaccio family. It is not surprising then that it welcomed artists from Flanders, Germany and even Sicily: Antonello da Messina stayed there in 1475 and 1476. The history of painting thus winds its way through trade, exchanges and journeys.

Antonello da Messina,
Christ at the Pillar,
Venice (?), circa 1476.
Oil on canvas, 29.8 x 21 cm.

Leonardo da Vinci, *Portrait of Lisa Gherardini del Giocondo*, known as *La Gioconda* or *Mona Lisa*, Florence, circa 1503-1506. Oil on wood, 77 x 53 cm.

CENTRING,
POSTURE AND
THE HORIZON

Having become a genre in their own right towards the end of the 15th century, portraits were sometimes of the Court or fulfilled a ceremonial function; they served to capture the features of the ladies of the aristocracy and the *Grande Bourgeoisie*, such as queens and humanists. Every kind of device would henceforth be implemented: favouring a particular angle of vision, close-up, wide view or depth of field; highlighting the posture of the models, an attitude suited to their body, or even their moral or psychological state; bringing out the figure on a neutral background; opening up the space through a loggia, and raising and bringing out the horizon.

△ Leonardo da Vinci,
*Portrait of a Lady
of the Milanese Court,*
Milan, circa 1485-1495.
Oil on wood, 63 x 45 cm.

◁ Leonardo da Vinci,
Portrait of Lisa Gherardini del Giocondo,
known as *La Gioconda* or *Mona Lisa,*
Florence, circa 1503-1506.
Oil on wood, 77 x 53 cm.

△ Above:
Hans Holbein, the Younger,
Anne of Cleves, London, 1539.
Oil on canvas, 65 x 48 cm.

△ Top left:
Paolo Caliari, known as Veronese,
The Beautiful Nani, Venice,
circa 1560. Oil on canvas,
119 x 103 cm.

△ Above:
Corneille de Lyon,
Louise de Rieux, circa 1550.
Oil on wood, 16.5 x 12.5 cm.

△ Top right:
Raffaello Sanzio, known as Raphael,
and Giulio Romano,
Joan of Aragon, Rome, 1518.
Oil on canvas, 120 x 95 cm.

△ Raffaello Sanzio, known as Raphael, *Balthazar Castiglione*,
Rome, 1514-1515. Oil on canvas, 82 x 67 cm.

Andrea del Sarto,
Holy Family with Angels,
Florence, circa 1515-1516.
Oil on wood, 141 x 108 cm.

Pietro Perugino,
Apollo and Marsyas,
Florence, circa 1495.
Oil on wood, 39 x 29 cm.

Italian painter,
Concert, Florence,
second half of the 16th century.
Oil on canvas, 180 x 131 cm.

Andrea Solario, *The Annunciation*, Milan, 1506. Oil on wood, 76 x 78 cm.

At the beginning of the century, Italy, both in Tuscany and Lombardy, honoured the iconographical codes inherited from the *Quattrocento*. Whether in the secular or religious domain, the stature of an Apollo or a Holy Family group had to be easy to distinguish. As regards the mystery of the Annunciation and the representation of Mary, the painter was obliged to choose from five preestablished "attitudes": turmoil - the Virgin is amazed; contemplation - she tries to understand; uncertainty - she asks questions; submission - she kneels, lowers her head and accepts her mission; and, lastly, merit - she is alone and will carry the child of God. In Milan, Andrea Solario was not unaware of this set of rules.

RAPHAEL

Raffaello Sanzio, known as Raphael,
Saint George Fighting the Dragon, Florence,
circa 1504. Oil on wood, 29.4 x 25.5 cm.

Raffaello Sanzio, known as Raphael, *The Virgin and Child
with Saint John the Baptist*, also known as *La Belle Jardinière*,
Florence, 1507. Oil on wood, 122 x 80 cm.

Having passed through the studio of Perugino and then worked in
Florence, Raphael was called to Rome in 1508 by Pope Julius II. He
was placed in charge of the official decoration of the Vatican, appointed architect of Saint Peter's Basilica, took charge of supervising the
city's antiquities, and surrounded himself with fellow artists and assistants - including Giulio Romano and Giovanni Francesco Penni. No
other was so esteemed or became such a legend in his own lifetime
as this painter, architect and antiquarian. The self-portrait that he
bequeathed in 1519, a year before his death at thirty-seven years of
age, reveals nothing of his greatness. Standing in the background,
Raphael rests his hand on the shoulder of a friend.

Raffaello Sanzio, known as Raphael, *Saint Michael*,
Florence, circa 1504. Oil on wood, 30.9 x 26.5 cm.

Raffaello Sanzio, known as Raphael, *Raphael and a Friend*, Rome, 1519. Oil on canvas, 99 x 83 cm.

THE DESTINY OF SAINT JOHN THE BAPTIST

John, known as the Baptist, was the son of Zechariah and Elizabeth. He was a prophet and forerunner for he announced the coming of the Messiah and foretold the destiny of Jesus whom he baptised in approximately 27 A.D. on the banks of the Jordan. By revealing the martyr's cross, he showed that he knew the Passion of Christ. John was thrown into prison for denouncing the incest committed by Herod Antipas who had married his brother's wife, Herodias. Salome, daughter of Herodias and Herod Philip, offered to dance for her uncle in return for the head of the prophet. The transformation of the tale into images, the unfolding of a narrative scene, the choice of momentum and the final deed are the responsibility of the artists.

△ Above: Lorenzo Sabatini,
The Virgin, the Child Jesus, and the Young Saint John the Baptist, Bologna, 1572. Oil on canvas, 173 x 142 cm.

△ Top: Lambert Sustris, known as Lambert of Amsterdam,
The Birth of Saint John the Baptist, Venice, 16th century. Oil on canvas, 96 x 128 cm.

△ Above: Studio of Raffaello Sanzio, known as Raphael, *Saint John the Baptist in the Desert Revealing the Cross of the Passion*, Rome, circa 1517. Oil on canvas, 135 x 142 cm.

△ Top: Leonardo da Vinci,
Saint John the Baptist, Italy, circa 1513-1516. Oil on wood, 69 x 57 cm.

◁Left:
Giannicola di Paolo,
*The Baptism
of Christ*,
fragment of a predella,
16th century. Oil
on wood, 44 x 87 cm.

◁Below left:
Jacopo de'Barbari,
*The Virgin
and Child between
Saint John the
Baptist and Saint
Abbé Anthony*,
known as *The Virgin
of the Fountain*,
Venice (?),
circa 1500-1515.
Oil on canvas,
47 x 55 cm.

◁Centre:
Giovanni Antonio
Boltraffio, *The Virgin
and Child with
Saint John the
Baptist and Saint
Sebastian between
Two Donors*, known
as *The Casio Family
Virgin*, Bologna,
1500. Oil on wood,
186 x 184 cm.

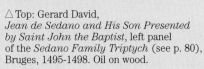

△Cornelis Van Haarlem,
The Baptism of Christ (detail),
Haarlem, 1588. Oil on wood.

△Bernardino Luini,
*Salome Receiving the Head
of Saint John the Baptist*,
Milan, pre-1532.
Oil on canvas, 62.5 x 55 cm.

△Above: Andrea Solario,
The Head of Saint John the Baptist,
Milan, 1507. Oil on wood, 46 x 43 cm.

△Top: Gerard David,
*Jean de Sedano and His Son Presented
by Saint John the Baptist*, left panel
of the *Sedano Family Triptych* (see p. 80),
Bruges, 1495-1498. Oil on wood.

GERARD DAVID

The "unequivocal master": Gerard David would in future be able to lay claim to this title as part of the Bruges Guild of painters in 1484. He was received by the aristocrats of the city and admitted as a member of an association which, according to a northern tradition, brought together proprietors - artisans, merchants or anyone united by the same trade. He was therefore granted the right to practise his occupation freely since, as a "master", he supervised a studio consisting of apprentices and journeymen. Through his marriage to Cornelia Cnoop, the daughter of the dean of the brotherhood of silversmiths, Gerard David occupied a notable place in the Flemish city on two accounts.

Gerard David, *God the Father Bestowing a Blessing*, Bruges, 1506. Oil on wood, 46 x 88 cm.

Gerard David, *Sedano Family Triptych: The Virgin and Child Flanked by Two Angelic Musicians* (central panel), *Jean de Sedano and His Son Presented by Saint John the Baptist* (left panel), *The Wife of Jean de Sedano Presented by Saint John* (right panel), Bruges, 1495-1498. Oil on wood, 97 x 145 cm.

Gerard David, *The Wedding at Cana*, Bruges, 1501-1502. Oil on wood, 100 x 128 cm.

JOOS VAN CLEVE, QUENTIN METSYS

Quentin Metsys,
The Virgin and Child,
Anvers, 1529.
Oil on wood, 68 x 51 cm.

Joos van Cleve,
The Lamentation of Christ,
central panel of an altarpiece,
Anvers, circa 1530.
Oil on wood, 145 x 206 cm.

Quentin Metsys,
*The Money-Lender
and His Wife*, Anvers, 1514.
Oil on wood, 70 x 67 cm.

Objects have innumerable, infinite roles within a painting. Joos van Cleve
and Quentin Metsys make brilliant use of them in different registers. A
sponge, a bowl, a skull and bones are positioned close to the body of Christ,
on the ground, once again telling of his suffering and death. A bunch of
grapes and its shadow, a knife placed diagonally next to a fig, a tablet or win-
dowsill in front of the Virgin create the illusion of the painting. As for the
mirror and the scales, the play of light on the bottle, the fruit and books on
the shelves, and the open door, these are so many elements which recons-
truct the image of a Flemish money-lender at the beginning of the 16th century, so many illusory or *trompe-l'œil* effects, and exercises in virtuosity.

THE LOW COUNTRIES

Jan Gossaert, known as Mabuse, *Carondelet Diptych:*
Jean Carondelet (left panel) and *Virgin and Child* (right panel),
Maubeuge, 1517. Oil on wood, 42 x 27 cm.

Master of the Repudiation of Hagar, *The Bearing of the Cross*,
Leyden, circa 1510-1520. Oil on wood, 85.5 x 60 cm.

What we now call "The Netherlands" is far from the territorial
reality of the 16th century. The Low Countries of the Renaissance
covered Holland, Friesland or Gelderland in the north, and
Flanders, Zeeland, Hainault or Brabant in the south. It was not
unusual for northern painters to settle in the cities of the south,
travelling from Leyden to Anvers - or vice versa. This equili-
brium was lost in 1579 when the Protestant north and Catholic
south were finally divided. Situated in the province of West
Flanders, Bruges is now part of Belgium; Maubeuge, a city in
the Hainault region, the "land of *La Haine*" or "hatred", is French;
and at the heart of southern Holland, Leyden is a city of The
Netherlands.

Lucas van Leyden, *The Fortune-teller*, Leyden, circa 1508.
Oil on wood, 24 x 30 cm.

Jan Provost, *Abraham, Sarah and the Angel*, Bruges, circa 1520. Oil on wood, 78.5 x 58 cm.

FROM BOSCH TO BRUEGEL

They paint worldly disorder. They create monsters, half-human and half-animal; they dream of strange scenes, scenes of madness; they study and depict the disabled, the deformed and the blind in intricate detail. The Devil is often involved since he conjures up an abundance of hallucinations, images of temptation, possession or infestation - in his retreat, a saint is persecuted by vagaries of nature. These are strategies which plunge the universe into anguish. Evil finds its amiable accomplices in the female sex, and summons its armies of witches, she-devils and sirens at will. Bosch, Pieter Huys and Bruegel - described as "another Bosch" by his contemporaries - are united by the portrayal of chaos.

Hieronymus Bosch, *The Ship of Fools*, Bois-le-Duc, circa 1500. Oil on wood, 58 x 32 cm.

Pieter Huys, *The Temptation of Saint Anthony*, Anvers, 1547. Oil on wood, 69.5 x 102 cm.

Pieter Bruegel, the Elder, *The Beggars*, Brussels, 1568. Oil on wood, 18 x 21 cm.

THE BIRTH OF THE LANDSCAPE:
OF NATURE
AND MEN

The background of greenery which framed the face of the Virgin or a scene of Lamentation gradually became transformed into a broader vision of the universe: an awareness of the landscape emerged in the 16th century, which raised rocks, valleys and lakes, and the effects of rain or a storm to the highest level. Studied, measured, placed in perspective, a reflection of religious sentiment or a frame of mind, nature achieved its autonomy.

▷ Top: Joachim Patinir, *Saint Jerome in the Desert*, Anvers, circa 1515. Oil on wood, 78 x 137 cm.

▷ Right: Painter from Anvers or Leyden, *Lot and His Daughters*, circa 1520. Oil on wood, 48 x 34 cm.

▷ Left: Barend van Orley, *Christ in the Olive Grove*, Anvers, circa 1519. Oil on wood, 89 x 66 cm.

△ Top left:
Lorenzo Lotto, *Saint Jerome in the Desert*, Venice, 1506. Oil on wood, 48 x 40 cm.

△ Top centre:
Simon Bening (attributed to), *Landscape with the Penitent Saint Jerome*, Bruges, pre-1561. Tempera on paper glued onto wood, 28.7 x 19.3 cm.

△ Top right: Wolf Huber, *The Lamentation of Christ*, Passau, 1524. Oil on wood, 105 x 87 cm.

△ Above left: Tiziano Vecellio, known as Titian, *Pastoral Concert*, Venice, circa 1510-1511. Oil on canvas, 110 x 138 cm.

△ Above: Niccolò dell'Abbate, *Moses Rescued from the Water*, Fontainebleau, 16th century. Oil on canvas, 82.5 x 83 cm.

◁ Left: Lucas van Valckenborch, *The Tower of Babel*, Flanders, 16th century. Oil on wood, 41 x 56.5 cm.

◁ Right: Ambrosius Benson, *Virgin and Child with Saint Barbara and Saint Catherine of Alexandria*, Bruges, 1530-1532. Oil on wood, 133 x 108 cm.

GERMAN SIGNATURES

Right: Hans Baldung Grien,
The Knight, the Young Girl and Death,
Nuremberg, circa 1505.
Oil on wood, 35.5 x 29.6 cm.

Below right:
Master HB of the Griffin Head,
Christ Blessing the Children,
Saxony, circa 1528-1553.
Oil on wood, 73 x 59 cm.

Below: Hans Sebald Beham,
The Story of David,
table platter, Frankfurt, 1534.
Oil on wood, 128 x 131 cm.

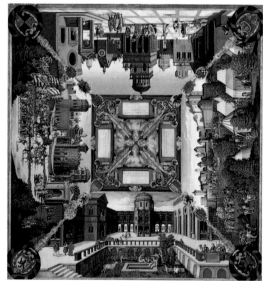

Lucas Cranach, the Elder, *Venus Standing in a Landscape*,
Wittenberg, 1529. Oil on wood, 38 x 25 cm.

Lucas Cranach, the Elder, *The Silver Age*,
formerly known as *The Effects of Jealousy*, Wittenberg, 1535.
Oil on wood, 77.5 x 52.5 cm.

Trained in Nuremberg, in southern Germany, Hans Baldung Grien
drew a small vine leaf at the bottom of his compositions and then chose
to add his initials, "HBG". In Wittenberg, in Saxony, Lucas Cranach
chose as his emblem a winged serpent which he intertwined with the
date of the painting - both in his *Venus*, by the veil falling onto the
ground, and in his illustration of Hesiod's poem, *Works and Days*. In
Nuremberg again, Albrecht Dürer marked his self-portraits with a
monogram, and sometimes inscribed a few lines. The painter, signing
and proudly presenting his effigy, had become an artist.

CRANACH, HOLBEIN

While Cranach the Elder was a painter in the court of the Electors of Saxony - Frederick III the Wise founded the University of Wittenberg and was a patron of Luther, Holbein the Younger executed numerous portraits of merchants, writers, men of the Church, scientists and ambassadors in Basle and then in London. His detail is observed in the silken fabrics, an embroidered mitre, and the velvet of a sleeve. He also endeavours to characterise a face and a function. Surely this is what one would expect from a portrait? In 1519, the painter called upon one of his paintings to speak: "I may be a painted image; I am not inferior to the living, but am like my master." Through this inscription, Holbein pays homage to his model and… to himself.

Studio of Lucas Cranach, the Elder, *Frederick III the Wise, Elector of Saxony* (1463-1525), Wittenberg, 1532. Oil on wood, 13.3 x 14.5 cm.

Lucas Cranach, the Elder, *Presumed Portrait of Magdalena Luther*, Wittenberg, circa 1540. Oil on wood, 41.1 x 26 cm.

Hans Holbein, the Younger, *William Warham*,
Archbishop of Canterbury in 1504, London, 1528.
Oil on wood, 82 x 66 cm.

Hans Holbein, the Younger, *Erasmus*, London, 1523.
Oil on wood, 42 x 32 cm.

Hans Holbein, the Younger,
Nicolas Kratzer, Basle, 1528.
Oil on wood, 83 x 67 cm.

CORREGGIO

A native of Correggio near Parma, Antonio Allegri applied himself to the spirit of each of his commissions, whether frescoes or devotional paintings created for religious institutions, or privately commissioned works reserved for the pleasure of a lord. Hence, a fantastic being, half-man, half-goat, plays the role of one who discovers and reveals Beauty and Love - is this the role of the painter or the onlooker? This Venus, startled in her sleep, was intended for Federico II Gonzaga, Duke of Mantua.

Antonio Allegri, known as Correggio, *The Mystical Marriage of Saint Catherine of Alexandria to Saint Sebastian*, Parma, circa 1526-1527. Oil on wood, 105 x 102 cm.

Antonio Allegri, known as Correggio, *Portrait of a Young Man (Self-portrait?)*, Parma, circa 1520-1530. Oil on wood, 59 x 44.3 cm.

Antonio Allegri, known as Correggio, *Venus, Satyr and Cupid*, Parma, circa 1524-1525. Oil on canvas, 188 x 125 cm.

MANNERISTS

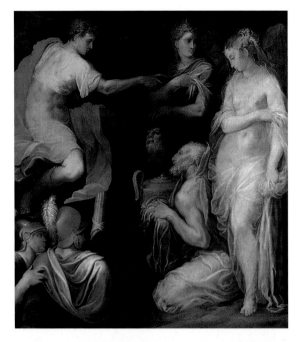

From the 1520's in Italy and then in France, artists adopted a "perfect manner", a "beautiful manner", a *bella maniera* based on "measure", "harmony" and "fantasy"... as described by the mannerist, Giorgio Vasari of Tuscany. In a Pietà, Rosso exaggerated the tension and stretching of forms, sought the disproportionate amplitude of the body, the broken folds and recesses, an astounding close-up, and the audacious harmony of orange juxtaposed with red. A century later, "mannerist" became an unfortunate synonym for "mannered" or affected, devoid of all that is natural. At the beginning of the 20th century, mannerism would even become part of psychiatric vocabulary, a term used to describe a disorder.

Niccolò dell'Abbate,
The Continence of Scipio,
Fontainebleau, circa 1556.
Oil on canvas, 127 x 115 cm.

Angelo di Cosimo, known as Bronzino, *Christ Appearing as a Gardener to Mary Magdalene*, or *Noli me tangere*, Florence, circa 1560. Oil on wood, 289 x 194 cm.

Jacopo Carucci, known as Pontormo, *The Virgin and Child with Saint Anne and Four Saints*, also known as *The Holy Conversation*, Florence, circa 1527-1529. Oil on wood, 228 x 176 cm.

Giovanni Battista di Jacopo, known as Rosso Fiorentino, *Pietà*, Fontainebleau, circa 1534-1540. Oil on wood transposed onto canvas, 127 x 163 cm.

THE CLOUET STUDIO

Jean Clouet was part of the king's household and, in 1516, counted among the valets of François I. A "manservant" or "valet" was thus a gentleman, an officer in one of the "services" revolving around the sovereign. While the "food service" included those presiding over the meals, from the head pantler in charge of supplying bread, to the head cupbearer in charge of wine, the "chamber service" denoted all those who came the closest to the sovereign. In 1528, Jean Clouet was promoted and became the official court painter, the king's first valet, paid to execute "portraits and effigies from life". He was succeeded by his son François in 1541.

Studio of François Clouet,
Charles IX, King of France (1550-1574),
Paris, circa 1560-1570. Oil on wood,
31.5 x 17 cm.

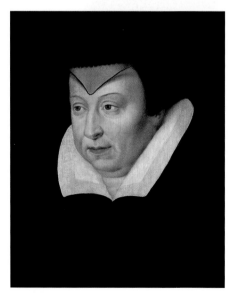

French painter, *Catherine de'Medici, Queen of France (1519-1589)*, Paris, circa 1580. Oil on wood, 30 x 25 cm.

Studio of François Clouet, *François de Lorraine, Duke of Guise (1519-1563)*, Paris, circa 1550-1560. Oil on wood, 31 x 23 cm.

François Clouet, *Elisabeth of Austria, Queen of France (1554-1592)*, Paris, circa 1571. Oil on wood, 36 x 26 cm.

Jean Clouet, *François I, King of France (1494-1547)*, Paris, circa 1530. Oil on wood, 96 x 74 cm.

FONTAINEBLEAU SCHOOL

Naked and draped in sensuality, the women created by the artists working at the Château de Fontainebleau seem to reappear in Pierre de Ronsard's *Loves*, which extols the beauty of the body in its most minute details, as can be seen in a sonnet dedicated to his beloved in 1555.
"Marie, your cheek is as fair
As a rose in May, your hair
Is the colour of chestnuts, its twisting coils
Gently curling around your ear. [...]
Your breasts are two mountains of curds,
Of the purest white on new rushes
Fashioned by a Maid in the month of June:
Juno gave you your arms, the Graces your breasts,
Aurora your hands and forehead,
But your heart, a proud lioness."

Fontainebleau School, *Charity*,
circa 1560. Oil on canvas, 147 x 96.5 cm.

·EVA·PRIMA·PANDORA·

Jean Cousin, the Elder, *Eva Prima Pandora*, Paris, circa 1550. Oil on wood, 97.5 x 150 cm.

Luca Penni (attributed to), *Diana the Huntress*, Fontainebleau, circa 1550. Oil on canvas, 191 x 132 cm.

HISTORY TOLD BY
BEAUTIFUL
HEROINES

They all offered their bodies to the Bible. Bathsheba was obliged to accept the tributes paid by King David, Susanna had to endure the stares of lustful old men, and Judith cut off the head of Holofernes, the enemy general. Another, a figure of Christian virtue, nursed the children of the Earth at her breast. Transformed into vain or innocent allegories, or smitten by a serpent, the women of the 16th century sacrificed themselves in order to incarnate history… Very few, however, left their name to a piece of work.

▷ Jan Massys,
David and Bathsheba,
Anvers, 1562.
Oil on wood,
162 x 197 cm.

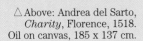

△ Above:
Jacopo Robusti,
known as Tintoretto,
Susanna Bathing,
Venice, 1550-1560.
Oil on canvas,
167 x 238 cm.

△ Top left:
Paolo Caliari,
known as Veronese,
*Susanna
and the Old Men*,
Venice, 16th century.
Oil on canvas,
198 x 198 cm.

△ Above: Andrea del Sarto,
Charity, Florence, 1518.
Oil on canvas, 185 x 137 cm.

△ Above centre:
Jan van der Straet,
Modesty Disarming Vanity,
Florence, 1569.
Oil on wood, 139 x 103 cm.

△ Above right: Jan Massys,
*Judith Holding the Head
of Holofernes*, Anvers,
after 1543. Oil on wood,
106 x 75 cm.

◁Left:
Giovanni Pedrini,
known as Gianpetrino,
*The Suicide
of Cleopatra
Bitten by an Asp*,
Milan, 16th century.
Oil on wood,
73 x 57 cm.

◁Right:
Bernardino Luini,
Silence,
San Sepolcro,
circa 1521.
Fragment of a fresco,
24 x 18 cm.

CORNEILLE DE LYON

Clément Marot, a poet patronised and admired by the Court, was in great danger in the Catholic 16th century. Denounced in 1526 for "eating bacon" during Lent, he was imprisoned in Châtelet. Suspected of heresy in 1534, accused of taking too close an interest in the ideas of the Reformation, he left the kingdom and sought refuge in Ferrara, and then in Venice. In order to return to France and regain favour with the king, he wrote an *Epistle* and finally renounced Protestantism in Lyons in 1536. Could this be him featured in one of the small portraits produced by the prosperous studio of a certain Corneille de Lyon? Eight years later, in 1544, Marot died in Turin, in exile.

Corneille de Lyon,
*Presumed Portrait
of Clément Marot*,
circa 1536. Oil on wood,
12 x 10 cm.

French Painter,
*Portrait of a Flautist
with One Eye*,
1566. Oil on wood,
62 x 50 cm.

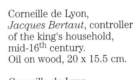

Corneille de Lyon,
Jacques Bertaut, controller
of the king's household,
mid-16th century.
Oil on wood, 20 x 15.5 cm.

Corneille de Lyon,
Pierre Aymeric,
merchant of Saint-Flour
then Consul of Lyons,
1533. Oil on wood,
16.5 x 14.2 cm.

TITIAN

Tiziano Vecellio, known as Titian, *The Entombment*, Venice, 1520-1522. Oil on canvas, 148 x 205 cm.

Tiziano Vecellio, known as Titian,
Man with Glove, Venice, 1520-1523.
Oil on canvas, 100 x 89 cm.

Tiziano Vecellio, known as Titian,
François I (1494-1547), Venice, 1538.
Oil on canvas, 109 x 89 cm.

While the Venetians of the Renaissance were taken with *colorito*, the Florentines swore only by *disegno*. It was a bitter struggle between colour and design, and both sides were irreconcilable. The debate continued the following century: in 1671, Philippe de Champaigne demonstrated before the Royal Academy the flawed appeal of colour, since "to study colour as the most important thing and to study colour alone would be to deceive oneself; it would be like choosing a beautiful body, allowing oneself to be dazzled by its splendour and ignoring that which alone animates this beautiful appearance, which cannot survive alone, however beautiful it may be, because beauty has no effect on the life of a body that is not sustained by the soul and spirit."

Tiziano Vecellio, known as Titian,
The Crowning with Thorns, Venice,
circa 1542. Oil on wood, 303 x 180 cm.

VENETIAN CANVASES

Based on oils and canvas, the aesthetics embraced by Venice make use of fluidity and the play of light. Having inherited a technique perfected the previous century by Flemish painters, the artists superimpose fine layers of pigment, apply transparent glazes, allowing the light to penetrate the painted surface and be reflected in the plaster covering the support. Canvas gradually came to replace frescoes and painted murals due to its greater resistance to the salty air and humid atmosphere of Venice. It would soon be the medium used in all easel paintings.

Lorenzo Lotto, *Christ and the Adulteress*, Venice, 1530-1535. Oil on canvas, 124 x 156 cm.

Lorenzo Lotto, *Christ Carrying His Cross*, Venice, 1526. Oil on canvas, 66 x 60 cm.

Paolo Caliari, known as Veronese, *The Pilgrims of Emmaus*, Venice, circa 1559-1560. Oil on canvas, 241 x 415 cm.

Studio of Paolo Caliari, known as Veronese, *Lot and His Family Fleeing Sodom*, Venice, after 1580. Oil on canvas, 93 x 120 cm.

TINTORETTO AND VERONESE

By achieving independence, by raising their status to that of creator, Renaissance painters demanded the right to solitude, secrecy and freedom, in the same way as intellectuals. Such was the case for Tintoretto and Veronese, two highly esteemed masters. When he was not painting, wrote Carlo Ridolfien in 1648, Jacopo Robusti "spent most of his time alone in his studio, which was in the remotest part of the house; in order to be able to see properly in his studio, he needed to have a light burning all day long. There, in the midst of innumerable sculptures, he would spend many hours owed to rest, arranging the models that he had made for the compositions on which his commissions were based [...]. And he would never allow other artists to watch him painting".

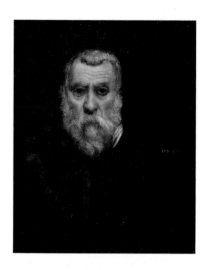

Jacopo Robusti, known as Tintoretto, *Self-Portrait*, Venice, circa 1587. Oil on canvas, 62.5 x 52 cm.

Jacopo Robusti, known as Tintoretto, *Paradise*, sketch for the Great Council Chamber, Ducal Palace of Venice, 1579-1580. Oil on canvas, 143 x 362 cm.

Paolo Caliari, known as Veronese, *The Wedding at Cana*, Venice, 1562-1563. Oil on canvas, 666 x 990 cm.

ARCIMBOLDO'S SEASONS

Greatly admired in the 16th century, *ghiribizzi* were "caricature techniques" to which painters merrily devoted themselves. Arcimboldo brilliantly devised all sorts of "composed heads", comical or astounding features, hideously contorted and unnatural. Blurring and parodying appearances, these allegories of the Seasons combine the ambiguity of the genres and the illusion of the form. Is that a nose or a gourd in the middle of the face? Is that an ear or a flower? And is that a pumpkin, a tree stump, or a tuft of hair?

Giuseppe Arcimboldo,
*Spring, Summer,
Autumn* and *Winter*,
Prague, 1573. Oil on canvas,
76 x 63.5 cm.
The floral borders
were added
in the 17th century.

EL GRECO AND SPAIN

Peeter de Kempeneer, known as Pedro Campaña,
Crucifixion, Seville, circa 1550.
Oil on canvas glued onto wood, 54 x 39 cm.

Juan de Borgoña, *The Virgin Supported
at the Foot of the Cross*, left panel of a triptych,
Toledo (?), circa 1515. Oil on wood, 134 x 106 cm.

When artists change countries, usually in search of patrons and
fortune, they also change their name, literally translating their
original surname or, conversely, choosing a nickname revealing
their origins. Peeter de Kempeneer left Flanders for Andalusia.
Cretan Domenikos Theotocopoulos was a native of Candia - now
Heraklion, which was placed under Venetian rule in the 16th
century. There he learned the two methods of painting: *alla
greca* followed the dictates of the Byzantine tradition with
gold backgrounds, while *alla italiana* adopted the new for-
mulas embraced by the Renaissance. Settling in Castile in
about 1577, El Greco worked on the elongated body and the
acidity of colour until his death.

Domenikos Theotocopoulos,
known as El Greco,
*Saint Louis, King of France,
and a Page*, Toledo, 1585-1590.
Oil on canvas, 120 x 96.5 cm.

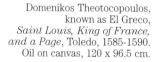

Fontainebleau School, *Gabrielle d'Estrées and One of Her Sisters*, circa 1595. Oil on wood, 96 x 125 cm.

The 16th century was punctuated with numerous diversions. Chariot processions, jousts, extravaganzas and comedies unfurled before ephemeral structures, mobile decorations devised by the official artists - Antoine Caron organised festivals and royal arrivals, thus celebrating the arrival of Henri III in Paris in 1573. Banquets and balls served to celebrate marriages. From the reign of Henri IV, who was nicknamed "*Vert Galant*", painting has preserved the memory of a number of mistresses, such as Gabrielle d'Estrées who died in 1599, leaving three children. In 1600, the marriage of Henri IV to Marie de' Medici of Florence opened the new century. The King was assassinated ten years later.

17th CENTURY

CARAVAGGIO

Darkness and falling shadows, *chiaroscuro*, the sudden transition from night to day: there was a great deal of scope for painters whose figures loomed out of the shadows or, on the contrary, were submerged in darkness. In Rome, at the very beginning of the 17th century, Caravaggio used shadows to harden volumes, to contrast without softening, to compose a tragic, human, painful image. A woman is laid out, and a shadow emphasises a lifeless hand, cuts across the folds of the dress covering her bloated, dead body. Sometimes the shadows reveal an invisible silhouette, a window outside the frame of the painting and, sweeping diagonally, bring to life the brownish background behind two figures.

Michelangelo Merisi, known as Caravaggio, *The Death of the Virgin*, painting rejected by the Carmelites of the Church of Santa Maria della Scala a Trastevere on the grounds of indecency, Rome, 1605-1606. Oil on canvas, 369 x 245 cm.

Follower of Michelangelo Merisi, known as Caravaggio, *Saint John the Baptist Holding a Sheep*, Italy, 17th century. Oil on canvas, 148 x 95 cm.

Annibale Carracci, *The Hunt*, Bologna, circa 1588. Oil on canvas, 136 x 253 cm.

Annibale Carracci, *Fishing*, Bologna, circa 1587-1588. Oil on canvas, 136 x 253 cm.

THE APPEAL OF ROME

Charles Mellin, *Roman Charity*, Rome,
circa 1627-1628. Oil on canvas, 96 x 73 cm.

Domenico Zampieri, known as Domenichino,
Saint Cecilia with an Angel Holding a Score,
Rome, 1623-1633. Oil on canvas, 156 x 108 cm.

At the beginning of the century, many artists came to Rome in search of princely support, papal commissions and inspiration by antiquity. With a population of approximately one hundred thousand, the city henceforth asserted itself as the flourishing capital of the Catholic Church, the Rome of the Counter-Reformation which, during the previous century, triumphed over the advance of Protestantism. The presence of painters served to confirm this victory, whether Italian artists, such as Caravaggio, Fetti up to 1614, Zampieri and Reni, the Bolognese pupils of the Carracci, or French artists Charles Mellin, Claude Gellée or Nicolas Poussin.

Domenico Fetti,
Melancholy, Mantua,
circa 1620. Oil on canvas,
171 x 128 cm.

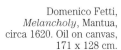

Guido Reni, *David, Vanquisher of Goliath*, Rome, 1603-1604. Oil on canvas, 220 x 145 cm.

IN THE FOOTSTEPS OF CARAVAGGIO

Claude Vignon, *The Young Singer*, Paris, circa 1622-1623.
Oil on canvas, 95 x 90 cm.

Hendrick Jansz, Terbrugghen, *The Duet*,
Utrecht, 1628. Oil on canvas, 106 x 82 cm.

Michael Sweerts, *The Young Man and the Go-between*, Rome, circa 1660.
Oil on copper, 19 x 27 cm.

Caravaggio had great influence in France, Holland and Italy. His concise half-length frames were taken up again, his use of the hands and expressions was admired, and musical and sensual scenes were dreamed up. The go-between and fortune-teller were prized subjects; known as an "Egyptian", a wily woman and deceiver, this "gypsy" tried to fool rich, naïve young men and women. Songs were dedicated to this colourful, erotic, edifying figure. In 1603, a madrigal by Gaspare Murtola thus pays homage to the Master, Caravaggio: "I know not who is the greatest magician / The woman whom you imitate / Or you who paints her / She is eager to steal from us / You make her painted image seem alive / Make others believe that she lives and breathes."

Nicolas Régnier, *The Fortune-teller*, Italy, circa 1625. Oil on canvas, 127 x 150 cm.

FRANS HALS

Frans Hals, *Jester with Lute*, Haarlem, pre-1626.
Oil on canvas, 70 x 62 cm.

Frans Hals (after), *Child with Soap-Bubble*, Haarlem, first half of the 17th century.
Oil on wood, d: 30 cm.

A deep-rooted tradition tends to associate the life and work of an artist, to link his very existence to the way in which he paints. A sober, reserved and brilliant man in society will be precise in his compositions, sensible in his method, and shrewd in his choice of subjects. The provocative, extravagant man who loves food and drink will display unbridled skill, a free and individual technique. This was how Frans Hal and his work were perceived: the vivid brushstrokes surely had to equate with this turbulent, indebted portraitist of jesters and prostitutes. However, the actual reality was undoubtedly more complex. The son of a weaver received commissions from the leading citizens of Haarlem, was celebrated and fairly well paid - even though he did not pay his baker, shoemaker or landlord, as shown by the numerous proceedings instituted against him.

Frans Hals, *The Gypsy*, Haarlem, 1630. Oil on wood, 58 x 52 cm.

VELVET BRUEGEL

Jan Bruegel I, known as Velvet Bruegel, *The Earth* or *Earthly Paradise*, Anvers, circa 1621.
Oil on wood, 45 x 65 cm.

Jan Bruegel I, known as Velvet Bruegel, *Air* or *Perspective*, Anvers, circa 1621. Oil on wood, 45 x 65 cm.

Jan Bruegel I, known as Velvet Bruegel, *The Battle of Issus*, formerly known as *The Battle of Arbela*, Anvers, 1602. Oil on wood, 80 x 136 cm.

Did Jan Bruegel's contemporaries consider his paintbrush to be so velvet-smooth that they gave him such a nickname? Or was it due to his elegance and his taste for velvet clothes that the son of Pieter Bruegel the Elder was thus described? It was down to Jan for having created a new genre, a lyrical landscape caught between the meticulous study and transcription of reality and the creation of a poetic imagination. Through the blues and greens that he arranged in the background, he created hazy horizons according to a fluid and finely shaded aerial perspective, whether painting the victory won by Alexander the Great against the Persian, Darius III Codoman, in 333 BC or composing the allegories of the four elements for the Ambrose Library in Milan.

RUBENS: THE MEDICI GALLERY

Peter Paul Rubens, *The Apotheosis of Henri IV and the Proclamation of the Regency of Marie de' Medici, 14 May 1610*, 14th painting in the cycle dedicated to Marie de' Medici, Anvers, 1621-1625. Oil on canvas, 394 x 727 cm.

Right:
Peter Paul Rubens,
*The Triumph
of Truth*,
24th painting in
the cycle dedicated
to Marie de' Medici,
Anvers, 1621-1625.
Oil on canvas,
394 x 160 cm.

Left:
Peter Paul Rubens,
*The Three Fates
Drawing out the
Destiny of Marie*,
4th painting in
the cycle dedicated
to Marie de' Medici,
Anvers, 1621-1625.
Oil on canvas,
394 x 155 cm.

Rubens and his studio undertook to portray the "highly illustrious life and heroic deeds of the Queen", Marie de' Medici, widow of Henri IV, Regent of France in 1610 and mother of Louis XIII, in twenty-eight paintings. This historical and political series, composed in an allegorical style, was destined for one of the galleries of the Palais du Luxembourg, the royal residence - which later became the Senate. "I confess to being more inclined to producing large works through a natural instinct rather than small curiosities," wrote the Master. "Each has his own gift; my talent is such that no undertaking, however vast in size or diversified in subject, has ever outmatched my courage." The cycle, executed in Anvers and completed in Paris, ended with *The Triumph of Truth*. Could this also describe the truthfulness to life of the painting?

Peter Paul Rubens, *The Arrival of Marie de' Medici at the Port of Marseille, 3 November 1600*,
9th painting in the cycle dedicated to Marie de' Medici, Anvers, 1621-1625. Oil on canvas, 394 x 295 cm.

DRAPED CLOTH
OR THE EXPRESSION
OF PASSION

The proportions of the body, its attitude, gestures and facial features are used by the artist to express the passions of the soul. Likewise, the way in which cloth is draped, the way in which it is made to embrace a movement or envelope the body, and the choice of striped or spotless material are processes conveying to the onlooker a thought, an emotion, or revealing a tragedy. Gentlemen make haste, accompanied by broken folds in reds and blues. Exhaustion takes hold, and the cloth spreads out and becomes intertwined. The painter uses draped cloth as a rhetorical figure.

▷ Peter Paul Rubens,
*The Apotheosis of Henri IV
and the Proclamation
of the Regency
of Marie de' Medici,
14 May 1610*
(detail, see p. 136),
Anvers, 1621-1625.
Oil on canvas.

▷ Right:
Gerard Seghers,
The Resurrection of Christ,
Anvers, circa 1620.
Oil on canvas, 324 x 240 cm

▷ Left:
Jacob Jordaens,
The Four Evangelists,
Anvers, 1617. Oil on canvas,
134 x 118 cm.

△Orazio Gentileschi, *The Repose of the Holy Family
during the Flight into Egypt*, Italy, circa 1628.
Oil on canvas, 157 x 225 cm.

△Guido Reni, *The Abduction of Helen*,
Bologna, 1631. Oil on canvas,
253 x 265 cm.

△Pietro Berrettini, known as
Pietro da Cortona, *Romulus and
Remus Given Shelter by Faustulus*,
Rome, circa 1643. Oil on canvas,
251 x 265 cm.

RUBENS' STUDIO

Right:
Peter Paul Rubens,
*Hélène Fourment
with a Carriage*,
Anvers, circa 1639.
Oil on wood,
195 x 132 cm.

Left:
Peter Paul Rubens,
*Hélène Fourment
and Her Children*,
Anvers, circa 1636.
Oil on wood,
115 x 85 cm.

Peter Paul Rubens, *The Raising of the Cross*, sketch, Anvers, 1609-1610. Oil on wood, 68 x 107 cm.

Jacob Jordaens, *Jesus Driving out the Merchants from the Temple*, Anvers, circa 1650. Oil on canvas, 288 x 436 cm.

"A large windowless room, lit only by an opening in the ceiling", such was the studio described by the Dane, Otto Sperling, passing through Anvers in 1621. "There were many young painters, all working on different canvases for which Rubens had prepared chalk sketches, indicating the colours here and there, and which he would subsequently finish himself." Alongside the Master worked not so much disciples but genuine collaborators, trained artists offering their expertise and specialist skills. Some would transform a sketch to a life-size drawing, namely Anthony van Dyck and Jacob Jordaens. Other artists, who were no less famous, were often entrusted with a section of the work: the borders of flowers would fall to Velvet Bruegel, and the still-lives and animals to Frans Snyders, while Jan Wildens would paint the landscapes. The whole piece would be executed under the watchful eye of Rubens.

FLEMISH SCENES

Peter Paul Rubens, *The Fair* or *Village Wedding*, Anvers, circa 1638. Oil on wood, 149 x 261 cm.

Country fairs, merry gatherings, the interiors of caba-
rets and studios are subjects which create an image of the
Flemish "genre painting". The actors are pipe-smokers,
revellers, and colour-grinders... In 17th century Flanders,
there was alcohol, beer, and tobacco: introduced into
Europe the previous century, it was taken as snuff, che-
wed, drunk as a decoction and occasionally mixed with
hemp. It was claimed to have great medicinal properties,
and when the diplomat Jean Nicot gave Catherine de'
Medici tobacco to ease her migraines, nicotine appeared
among us... While the protagonists of these "genre scenes"
came to sit in the painter's studio, collectors amassed
paintings of more "dignified" subjects in their curio collections. The cycle was thus complete.

David Teniers II, the Younger, *Man Smoking, Leaning
on a Table*, Anvers, 1643. Oil on canvas, 39 x 30.5 cm.

David Ryckaert III, *Studio Interior*, Anvers, 1638. Oil on wood, 59 x 95 cm.

Studio of Frans Francken II, the Younger, *Ulysses Recognising Achilles Among the Daughters of Lycomedes*, Anvers, 17th century. Oil on wood, 74 x 105 cm.

VAN DYCK

Invited to London in 1632, Anthony van Dyck left Anvers, was awarded a pension by Charles I, accepted as the "chief ordinary painter of Their Majesties" and made a knight. He devoted his last nine years, until his death in 1641, to four hundred portraits. Majestic figures, members of the English aristocracy and the play of light on a white shirt in a landscape followed one after another. After several visits to the Louvre, Marcel Proust dedicated a few lines to the Duke of Richmond: "You rejoice, van Dyck, prince of quiet gestures, / In all the beautiful beings who are soon to die, / In each beautiful hand which still knows how to open" (*Portraits of painters*, 1891).

Anthony van Dyck, *Charles I, King of England, Out Hunting (1625-1649)*, London, 1635-1638. Oil on canvas, 266 x 207 cm.

Anthony van Dyck, *Princes Palatine Charles Louis I, Elector, and His Brother Robert*, London, 1637. Oil on canvas, 132 x 152 cm.

Anthony van Dyck, *Venus Asking Vulcan for Arms for Aeneas*, Anvers, circa 1630. Oil on canvas, 220 x 145 cm.

Anthony van Dyck, *James Stuart, Duke of Lennox and Richmond*, London, circa 1632-1641. Oil on canvas, 107 x 84 cm.

FRENCH PAINTERS 1620-1650

Above: Jacques Blanchard, *Venus and the Graces Startled by a Mortal*, Paris, 1631-1633. Oil on canvas, 170 x 218 cm.

Left: Simon Vouet, *The Presentation in the Temple*, Paris, circa 1630-1635. Oil on canvas, 393 x 250 cm.

Below: Louis or Antoine Le Nain, *Peasant Family in an Interior*, Paris, circa 1640-1645. Oil on canvas, 113 x 159 cm.

Laurent de La Hyre,
The Dead Adonis and His Dog,
Paris, circa 1624-1628.
Oil on canvas, 109 x 148 cm.

From the end of the Regency of Marie de' Medici to the death of Louis XIII in 1643, and from the Regency of Anne of Austria to the personal reign of Louis XIV in 1661, French painting nurtured diversified styles, all marked by a sense of space, tragedy and poetry: architectural scenography appealed to Simon Vouet, the art of revealing suggested Jacques Blanchard, the solemnity of everyday life was the work of the Le Nain brothers, the portrayal of History, Music and Comedy became Eustache Le Sueur, and the vision of La Hyre was startling, with extreme foreshortening revealing the beauty of a body, that of Adonis, whose blood mingled with nectar to bring forth an anemone.

Eustache Le Sueur, *Clio, Euterpe and Thalia*,
part of the décor in the Muses Chamber of the
Residence of President Nicolas Lambert de Thorigny,
Paris, 1652-1655. Oil on canvas, 130 x 130 cm.

GEORGES DE LA TOUR

Georges de La Tour, *The Adoration of the Shepherds*, Lunéville, after 1640. Oil on canvas, 107 x 131 cm.

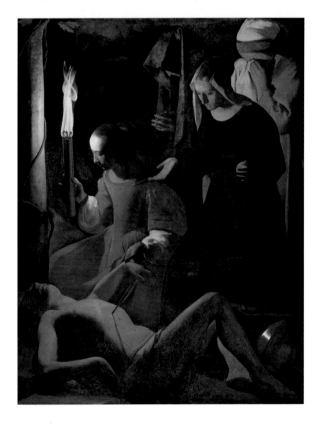

There are at least three sources, three images of light: one may be spiritual, another arises from the lighting, and the third belongs to the painters. The Latin *lux* signifies both the brilliant, active light of the divine, and the bright light of day. Those named Lucy or Lucian were born "before or with the light of day", and it was Lucifer who "carried the light" before becoming master of the fallen angels. The word *lumen* describes all kinds of light, whether emanating from a candlestick or representing the light of the eyes. The light of La Tour is without a doubt all of this at the same time, the flame of a torch piercing the darkness, shining through a hand, radiating in the body of an infant.

Georges de La Tour,
Saint Sebastian Tended by Saint Irene,
Lunéville, 1649. Oil on canvas, 167 x 131 cm.

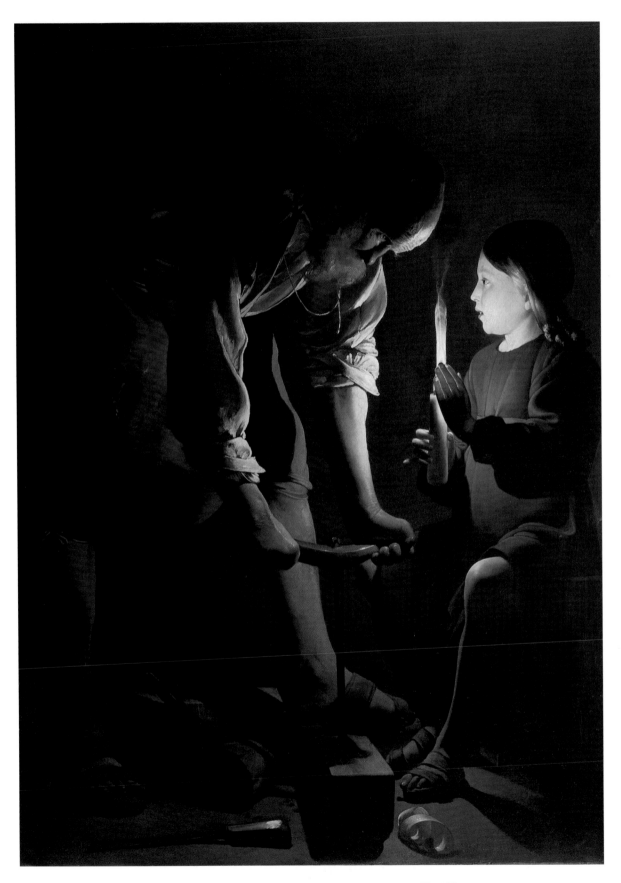

Georges de La Tour, *Saint Joseph the Carpenter*, Lunéville, circa 1640. Oil on canvas, 137 x 102 cm.

149

GAMBLERS
AND ARTISTS,
THE SONS OF SATURN

Reigning over melancholy, Saturn governs the destiny of gamblers and artists. Possessed by gambling and smitten by painting, they are all subjected to the influence of the planet which, in times past, symbolised the son of Jupiter and the god of Time. Together, they are marked by this "melancholy", this "black bile", one of the four humours defined by Hippocrates along with blood, phlegm and yellow bile. Short-tempered, over-sensitive, eccentric, eternally sorrowful, and solitary, but also passionate, gifted with talent or even genius, such are the poor wretches cursed with a saturnine temperament: skilled at cards or rolling the dice, and masters in the execution of a painting. In the 17th century, the melancholic figure went out of fashion. Two centuries later, it would return to haunt the romantics.

▷ Georges de La Tour,
Cheat with the Ace of Diamonds,
Lunéville, circa 1635.
Oil on canvas, 107 x 146 cm.

▷ Antoine Le Nain (attributed to),
The Young Card Players,
Paris, 17th century.
Oil on copper, 15 x 17.5 cm.

◁ Left:
Laurent de La Hyre,
The Game of Dice,
known as *Misfortune*,
Paris, pre-1630.
Oil on canvas,
127 x 109 cm.

◁ Centre:
Pieter de Hooch,
The Card Players,
Delft, 17th century.
Oil on wood,
60 x 49 cm.

△ Top right:
David Teniers II,
known as the Younger,
*Cabaret Interior:
The Game of Cards*,
Anvers, 1645.
Oil on canvas,
57.5 x 77.5 cm.

◁ Left:
Mathieu Le Nain
(attributed to),
*The Game
of Backgammon*,
Paris, 17th century.
Oil on canvas,
96 x 123 cm.

△ Above:
French painter, *Vanitas*,
circa 1650. Oil on canvas,
72 x 90 cm.

◁ Left:
Dirck van Delen,
The Game of Skittles,
Arnemuiden, 1637.
Oil on canvas, 85 x 145 cm.

◁ Bottom left:
Dirck van Delen,
The Tennis Players,
Arnemuiden, 1626.
Oil on wood, 32 x 54 cm.

◁ Right: Gerrit Lundens,
Blind Man's Buff,
Holland, 17th century.
Oil on wood, 78 x 69 cm.

NICOLAS POUSSIN: POETRY

Nicolas Poussin, *The Shepherds of Arcadia*, Rome, circa 1638-1640. Oil on canvas, 85 x 121 cm.

Each theme has its own type of representation. Nicolas Poussin's letter to Paul Fréart de Chantelou on 24 November 1647, aimed to convince the collector that this variation of styles was indeed valid: "Skilled poets have taken extreme care and used ingenious devices to fit the words in a line and to arrange metrical feet according to speech. Since Virgil studies his poems in detail, because he adapts the very sound of the verse to each of his three manners of speech with such great ingenuity, through the sound of the words, he appears literally to conjure up before your very eyes the subject with which he is dealing, such that where he speaks of love, one can see that he has artfully chosen no graceful, soft words pleasing to the ears". The painter is just like the poet.

Nicolas Poussin, *Echo and Narcissus*, Rome, circa 1628-1630. Oil on canvas, 74 x 100 cm.

Nicolas Poussin, *The Inspiration of the Poet*, Rome, circa 1630. Oil on canvas, 182 x 213 cm.

"GOD OF THE UNDERWORLD, RESTORE THIS RARE BEAUTY"

"Eurydice is no more, but my fire still burns.
This nascent flower, only just in bloom.
Alas! In her most wondrous spring
A serpent ended her sad destiny,
Just as through sweet marriage
She my constant fire was to reward.
Oh! Allow your hand to touch my extreme pain,
God of the Underworld, restore this rare beauty,
Day to me is odious without my beloved nymph,
Restore her to life or take away my light."

Orpheus pleading with Pluto,
Orpheus' Descent into the Underworld,
anonymous libretto,
opera by Marc Antoine Charpentier, 1686

▷ Nicolas Poussin,
Landscape with Orpheus and Eurydice,
Rome, circa 1650.
Oil on canvas, 124 x 200 cm.

Orpheus, Aeneas, Pollux, Theseus, Psyche... There is a long list of princes, lovers, heroes and heroines who descended into the underworld. Embarking upon their journey into that deep beyond, they disturb the abode of the deceased, reigned over by Pluto and Proserpine, guarded by Cerberus the monster, and where Charon the boatman ferries the shadowy figures on his boat. In Christian iconography, the dead may also take on the form of a shadowy figure.

△ Above:
Cornelis van Poelenburgh, *Orpheus Playing the Violin at the Entrance to the Underworld*, Utrecht, 17th century. Oil on wood, 38.5 x 47.5 cm.

△ Top:
François Perrier, *Orpheus Singing Before Pluto and Proserpine*, Paris, circa 1647-1650. Oil on canvas, 54 x 70 cm.

△ Above:
François Perrier, *Aeneas and His Companions Fighting the Harpies*, Paris, circa 1646-1647. Oil on canvas, 155 x 218 cm.
At the entrance to the Underworld, the Harpies steal the souls from the dead.

△ Top:
Roelant Savery, *Orpheus Charming the Animals*, Utrecht, 17th century. Oil on wood, 32 x 42 cm.

◁ Left:
Salvator Rosa, *The Ghost of Samuel Appearing to Saul*, Rome, 1668. Oil on canvas, 275 x 191 cm.

Nicolas Poussin, *The Plague of Ashdod*, Rome, 1630. Oil on canvas, 148 x 198 cm.

Nicolas Poussin, *Moses Rescued from the Water*, Rome, 1638. Oil on canvas, 93.5 x 121 cm.

Nicolas Poussin, *The Rape of the Sabine Women*, circa 1637-1638. Oil on canvas, 159 x 206 cm.

In order to work out his historical compositions, Poussin developed a series of studies. He would first study the geometrical structure. Using a metal stylet, he would draw out the perspective on the prepared coloured canvas - usually red or brown-ochre, he would choose a single or sometimes double vanishing point, arrange the parallel, orthogonal and transverse lines, and finally position the figures. According to a tradition going back to antiquity, the artist would arrange small waxen figures clothed in wet paper or fabric on a draughtboard, sometimes even using models with movable joints. This device would help him to observe the subtle proportions, foreshortenings, the effects arising from the space and the light, and the hang of the cloth... The painted sketch would then follow.

Nicolas Poussin, *Eliezer and Rebecca*, Rome, 1648. Oil on canvas, 118 x 199 cm.

CLAUDE GELLÉE, KNOWN AS LE LORRAIN

Claude Gellée, known as Le Lorrain, *The Village Fete*, Rome, 1639. Oil on canvas, 103 x 135 cm.

Are forgeries the price of success? Without a doubt, and artists are sometimes forced to use various stratagems in order to protect their work and assert their authenticity. Claude Gellée was a victim of the plagiarism abounding in Rome: other painters imitated his style, compositions and light, and managed to fool collectors. Hence at the end of the 17th century, according to Filippo Baldinucci, "he decided to create a compendium, and started to copy the inventions for each painting that he had sold, expressing each intricate detail of the painting itself, with a truly brilliant touch, also noting the name of the person for whom it had been commissioned and, if I remember rightly, the price it had fetched. He called this book the *Libro d'invenzioni, ovvero Libro di Vérità*". Using wash tints, Claude composed his own "Book of Truth".

Claude Gellée, known as Le Lorrain, *Cleopatra Disembarking at Tarsus*, Rome, 1642-1643. Oil on canvas, 119 x 170 cm.

Claude Gellée, known as Le Lorrain, *Ulysses Returning Chryseis to Her Father*, Rome, 1648. Oil on canvas, 56 x 72 cm.

Claude Gellée, known as Le Lorrain, *Sea Port, Misty Effect*, Rome, 1646. Oil on canvas, 119 x 150 cm.

CITIES OF THE UNITED PROVINCES

Jan Josephs van Goyen, *View of Dordrecht Downstream from the Grote Kerk*,
The Hague, 1647. Oil on wood, 74 x 108 cm.

In the 17th century, the United Provinces were formed into a republic which was to be declared, despite the continuous conflicts setting them against the Lower Countries of the South which remained in the hands of the Spanish. The brand new republic grew in wealth, both in its own territory and in the rest of the world. By creating an East India company in 1602, it opened maritime trading posts, built shipyards, developed the merchant navy, imported raw materials and transformed its cities into powerful banking and economic centres. The port of Amsterdam was one of the largest in Europe, and in the new stock market, built in the city in 1608, all kinds of commodities from wheat to herrings and cinnamon to tulip bulbs were negotiated and speculated upon. This new prosperity also won over the art market.

Pieter Jansz. Saenredam, *Interior of the Church of Saint Bavon in Haarlem*, Haarlem, 1630. Oil on wood, 41 x 37 cm.

Gabriel Metsu, *The Amsterdam Vegetable Market*, Amsterdam, circa 1658-1660. Oil on canvas, 97 x 84 cm.

Pieter de Hooch, *Woman Drinking*, Delft, 1658. Oil on canvas, 69 x 60 cm.

CONCERTS IN HOLLAND

Gerard Ter Borch,
*The Duet: Singer
and Theorbist,*
Holland, circa 1660-1669.
Oil on canvas, 82.5 x 72 cm.

Gabriel Metsu,
The Virginal Lesson,
Amsterdam, 17th century.
Oil on wood, 32 x 24.5 cm.

Where is the beauty in music? What is pleasing to the ears? A single voice or a concert? It all depends on the taste of the listener, wrote René Descartes, while in Amsterdam, in a letter to Marin Mersenne, on 18 March 1630: "the same thing that makes some people want to dance can make others want to cry. This stems from the rekindling of thoughts in our memory: for example, those who once took pleasure in dancing when a certain tune was playing, as soon as they hear a similar tune, immediately long to dance again. On the contrary, if someone had never before heard a galliard being played and if at the same time they were suffering from some sort of affliction, they would inevitably be saddened on hearing it again. I would imagine that one thing is certain: if a dog is whipped several times to the sound of the violin, as soon as it hears this music again, it would start to whimper and run away".

Gerard Ter Borch,
*The Concert: Singer
and Theorbist*,
Holland, circa 1657.
Oil on wood, 47.1 x 44 cm.

Caspar Netscher,
The Viola da Gamba Lesson,
The Hague, 1667.
Oil on wood, 44 x 35.5 cm.

Gerard Dou, *Woman Hanging a Cock*,
known as *The Dutch Housewife*,
Leyden, 1650. Oil on wood, 26.1 x 20.7 cm.

Willem van Mieris, *The Game Seller*, Leyden,
end of the 17th century. Oil on wood, 31 x 26.5 cm.

The Dutch art market was not simply flourishing but saturated, predominantly with small
paintings, genre scenes and portraits of everyday life. A second trade was sometimes essential for an artist. While Rembrandt and Vermeer
worked in the art business, Jan Steen kept a
brewery in Delft and a tavern in Leyden, and
Jacob van Ruisdael practised as a barber-sur-
geon. Some survived and received all kinds of
goods in payment for their work, whereas others
made their fortune, such as Gerard Dou, who
became the master of a "minute style", negotiated small fortunes for his work, and set his
tariff according to the number of hours involved.
Others went bankrupt, such as Rembrandt, forced in 1656 to sell all of his possessions, his collections and home, at the age of fifty.

Jan Steen,
Family Meal,
Leyden, pre-1679.
Oil on canvas,
82 x 68.5 cm.

Rembrandt Harmensz van Rijn, *The Flayed Ox*, Amsterdam, 1655. Oil on wood, 94 x 69 cm.

REMBRANDT AND CHIAROSCURO

Chiaroscuro is a pictorial technique used to create the illusion and relief of forms, as described in Antoine Furetière's *Universal Dictionary* in 1690: "Light, in terms of Painting, describes those areas which reflect light the most, and which are composed of the highest, most vivid colours. The science of the Painter is to manage skilfully the *light* in a painting, the colours, the shades and the recesses. The Painter clearly understands *chiaroscuro* to mean that he gives his figures great depth, that he extricates and brings them out by means of light and shade." Rembrandt constructed his faces in the golden softness of shadowy light.

Rembrandt, *Portrait of Titus,
Son of the Artist*, Amsterdam,
circa 1660. Oil on canvas, 72 x 56 cm.

Rembrandt Harmensz van Rijn,
Portrait of the Artist at His Easel,
Amsterdam, 1660.
Oil on canvas, 111 x 90 cm.

Rembrandt Harmensz
van Rijn, *Philosopher
Deep in Thought*,
Amsterdam, 1632.
Oil on wood,
28 x 34 cm.

Rembrandt Harmensz
van Rijn, *The Pilgrims
at Emmaus*, Amsterdam,
1648. Oil on wood,
68 x 65 cm.

ON REMBRANDT'S BATHSHEBA

Salomon de Bray, *Young Girl Dressing Her Hair*, Haarlem, circa 1630. Oil on wood, 54 x 46 cm.

Govert Flinck,
*Young Girl Dressed
as a Shepherdess*,
Amsterdam, 1641.
Oil on canvas, 71 x 65 cm.

Bathsheba's body was coveted and possessed by King David, according to the second book of Samuel in the Old Testament. From a monochrome outline painted with a brush, on scarcely perceptible, darkened backgrounds without much use of pigments, Rembrandt modelled the flesh and tissues in luminous layers of white and yellow impasto. This technique would be despised by some as simply amounting to mud on coarse canvas. Two centuries later, the blacks, the shades and the hands would fascinate van Gogh: "I especially admired Rembrandt's and Hals' hands, hands that were alive, but not "finished", according to the meaning that one would now like to give by force to the word "finish"", he wrote in October 1885. In the first half of the 17th century, Holland proposed other Bathshebas, other painted bodies.

Willem Drost, *Bathsheba Receiving the Letter from David*, Amsterdam, 1654. Oil on canvas, 103 x 87 cm.

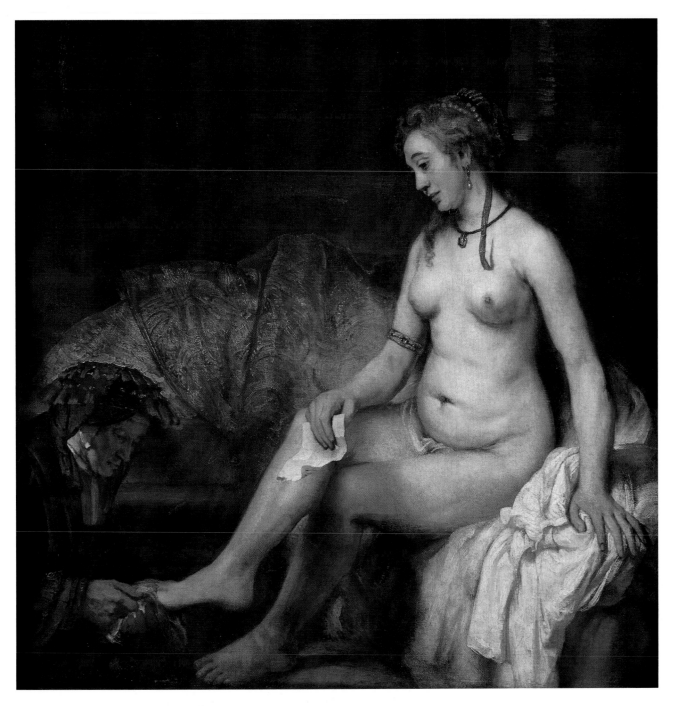

Rembrandt Harmensz van Rijn, *Bathsheba Bathing*, Amsterdam, 1654. Oil on canvas, 68 x 65 cm.

"A MATERIAL THING, SET DOWN BETWEEN THE LEAVES OF BOOKS"

"While, for us, reading is the inciter whose magical keys open up the door to dwellings in our innermost being where we have not yet dared to tread, it has a beneficial role in our lives. It becomes dangerous, however, when reading tends to replace rather than awaken us to the individual life of the mind, when we no longer perceive the truth as an ideal that can only be attained by the intimate progress of our thoughts and by the effort of our heart, but as a material thing, set down between the leaves of books, like honey made by others which we only need trouble ourselves to take down from the library shelves and then taste passively, with our body and mind in perfect repose."

Marcel Proust, *On Reading*, 1905.

◁Georges de La Tour,
*Mary Magdalene
by a Night-Light*, Lunéville,
circa 1640-1645.
Oil on canvas, 128 x 94 cm.

◁Right:
Gerard Ter Borch,
The Reading Lesson,
Holland, circa 1652.
Oil on wood, 27 x 25.3 cm.

◁Left:
Gerard Dou, *Old Woman:
Rembrandt's Mother*,
Leyden, 17th century.
Oil on wood, 12.5 x 9.4 cm.

△ Above:
Salomon Koninck
(attributed to), *Philosopher
with an Open Book*,
Amsterdam, circa 1633.
Oil on wood, 28 x 33.5 cm.

△ Top left:
Gerard Dou, *The Bible
Reading*, Leyden,
17th century. Oil on wood,
60.4 x 46 cm.

△ Top centre:
Gerard Dou,
Hermit Reading, Leyden,
1661. Oil on wood,
23 x 18.7 cm.

△ Above:
Philippe de Champaigne
(attributed to), *Portrait
of a Man*, Paris, 17th century.
Oil on canvas, 88 x 68 cm.

△ Above left:
Georges de La Tour (after),
Saint Jerome Reading,
France, 17th century.
Oil on canvas, 122 x 93 cm.

△ Above centre:
Adriaen van Ostade,
Man Reading at the Window,
Haarlem, 17th century.
Oil on wood, 26.6 x 21.8 cm.

△ Sébastien Stoskopff, *Books, Candle
and Bronze Statuette*, Paris or Strasbourg,
17th century. Oil on canvas, 51 x 69 cm.

△ Sébastien Stoskopff (attributed to),
Skull with Sundial, Paris or Strasbourg,
circa 1626-1640. Oil on canvas, 67 x 86 cm.

VERMEER, THE LACEMAKER AND OTHER OCCUPATIONS

Gerard Dou, *The Tooth-Drawer*, Leyden, 17th century.
Oil on wood, 32 x 26.3 cm.

Adriaen van Ostade, *The Schoolmaster*, Haarlem, 1662.
Oil on wood, 40 x 32.5 cm.

Picturesque, narrative and true to life, the images of everyday life in Delft, Amsterdam, Leyden and elsewhere are continual exercises in structure, colour and matter. The tooth-drawer allows us to glimpse a collection of objects, a skull, a reflection, a ray of light; the schoolmaster is at the centre of overlapping spaces; the reveller, she who likes to make merry, who loves to drink, is surrounded by textural effects. The lacemaker, Vermeer's smallest painting, focuses so precisely on the droplets and coloured thread.

Gabriel Metsu, *The Reveller*, Amsterdam,
17th century. Oil on wood, 28 x 27 cm.

△ Top left:
Jan Fyt, *Game and Hunting
Gear Discovered by a Cat*,
Anvers, circa 1640-1650.
Oil on canvas, 95 x 122 cm.

△ Top centre:
Peter Paul Rubens,
*Philopoemen, General
of the Achaeans, Recognised
by His Hosts at Megara*,
Anvers, circa 1610.
Oil on wood, 50 x 66 cm.

△ Top right:
Studio of Frans Snyders,
*The Fishmongers
at Their Stall*,
Anvers, after 1621.
Oil on canvas, 210 x 342 cm.

△ Above left:
Louise Moillon, *The Fruit
and Vegetable Seller*,
Paris, 1630. Oil on canvas,
120 x 165 cm.

△ Above right:
Louise Moillon,
*Bowl of Cherries, Plums
and Melon*, Paris, 1633.
Oil on canvas, 48 x 65 cm.

△ Above: Pierre Dupuis,
*Plums and Peaches
on a Mantelpiece*, Paris,
1650. Oil on canvas,
51 x 60 cm.

△ Above right:
Paul Liégeois, *Peaches, Plums
and Grapes*, France, circa 1650.
Oil on canvas glued
onto cardboard, 25 x 37 cm

△ Lubin Baugin, *Still Life with Chessboard*,
Paris, pre-1663. Oil on wood, 55 x 73 cm.

△ Michel Boyer, *Double Bass, Music Book
and Sword*, Paris, 1693. Oil on canvas, 81 x 99 cm.

HERRERA, ZURBARÁN

In the 19th century, Spain sought notoriety and became fashionable, and Francisco de Zurbarán emerged as one of Seville's greatest painters. His monastic series, his portrayal of saints, his compositions and austerity all won favour with the romantics. When Delacroix stood before one of the Spaniard's paintings in 1832, Théophile Gautier recounted the charm of the martyrs wearing aristocratic dress. "These are the most delightful and romantic creatures that one could ever dream of," he ardently declared on 24 September 1837, "they look like costumes for one of Shakespeare's comedies." Both imposing and charming, they fix their gaze upon us while holding the instrument or object of their torture: Agatha carries her breasts on a platter and Lucy her eyes, Margaret stands next to a dragon, and Apollinia holds a pair of pincers.

Francisco de Herrera, the Elder, *Saint Basil Dictating His Doctrine*, Seville, circa 1639. Oil on canvas, 243 x 194 cm.

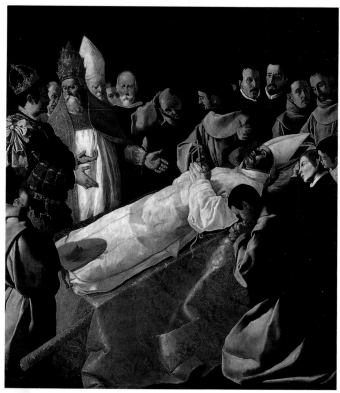

Francisco de Zurbarán, *The Lying in State of the Body of Saint Bonaventure*, Seville, circa 1629. Oil on canvas, 245 x 220 cm.

Francisco de Zurbarán, *Saint Apollinia*, Seville, circa 1636. Oil on canvas, 134 x 67 cm.

RIBERA, MURILLO

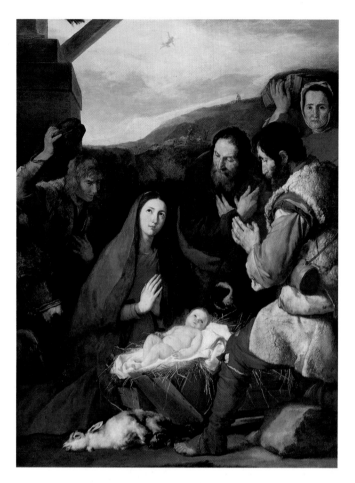

Jusepe de Ribera, *Adoration of the Shepherds*,
Naples, 1650. Oil on canvas, 239 x 181 cm.

An adventurer and wanderer, often a manservant or kit-
chen boy, sometimes a flea-ridden beggar and, if neces-
sary, a thief and a swindler, the *pícaro* was born in 16th
century Hispanic literature and experienced great fortune the following century. Often with an *hidalgo* as his
sworn enemy - a well-born man who places honour above
everything - the hero of "picaresque" novels considered
the whole of Europe a stage, soon making the transfer
from the written form to the painting. Solitary or part of
a group, the smiling or sometimes pitiful street urchin
became a stylistic device prized by collectors in Naples
and Seville. Working to both religious and secular commissions, Ribera and Murillo became masters in these portraits of children.

Jusepe de Ribera, *Boy with Club-Foot*, Naples, 1642.
Oil on canvas, 164 x 93 cm.

Bartolomé Esteban Murillo, *The Beggar Boy*, Seville, circa 1650. Oil on canvas, 134 x 110 cm.

PHILIPPE DE CHAMPAIGNE

Philippe de Champaigne,
Portrait of a Man, Paris, 1650.
Oil on canvas, 91 x 72 cm.

Philippe de Champaigne (attributed to),
Portrait of Two Men,
known as *Portrait of François Mansard
and Claude Perrault*, Paris, 1656.
Oil on canvas, 88 x 117 cm.

His hand rests on what would appear to be a window ledge, and his fingers cut across a misleading shadow; his sleeve falls not far from a chip in the stone; intermediary figures, boatmen, two architects plant themselves between our gaze and the structure of the painting. The painting is thus transformed into an open window; it is a space looking out upon our world; it becomes the place from which the figure has been taken. Linked with the Jansenist circle of the *Abbaye de Port-Royal-des-Champs* from 1646, Philippe de Champaigne elegantly used the illusion of portraiture.

Philippe de Champaigne, *The Apostle Philip*, Paris, 1649.
Oil on canvas, 117 x 89 cm.

Philippe de Champaigne, *The Dead Christ Lying on His Shroud*, Paris, pre-1654. Oil on wood, 68 x 197 cm.

LE BRUN, VAN DER MEULEN, PARROCEL

Charles Le Brun, *The Battle of Arbela*, sequel to *The History of Alexander*, Paris, 1669. Oil on canvas, 470 x 1264 cm.

"Chief painter to the king" in 1664, and enjoying absolute power, Charles Le Brun dedicated four monumental paintings to the history of Alexander. Appointed "painter of the conquests of the king", van der Meulen followed Louis XIV in his campaigns and sometimes portrayed his hunts and ceremonies. Parrocel was awarded a commission for eleven paintings on a military theme for the sovereign's dining room at the Château de Versailles. All three painters contributed to the emergence of a genre: the battle scene. Equipped with iconographical rules - how to represent a hero and how to portray the king as a hero -, it was displayed on a large scale in the galleries, favoured friezes or overhanging views, and connected the protagonists with the landscape.

Adam Frans van der Meulen,
View of the Château de Vincenr
or *Louis XIV Setting Out
for the Hunt*, Paris,
end of the 17th century.
Oil on canvas, 96 x 126 cm.

Joseph Parrocel, *Army of Louis XIV crossing the Rhine, at Tholhuis, on 12 June 1672*, Marly, 1699. Oil on canvas, 234 x 164 cm.

THE SELF-PORTRAIT:
THE SERENE MAJESTY
OF THE PAINTER

The 17th century in France was the age of glory. From then on, painters would pose at their ease, surround themselves with the attributes of their art and their official function, exaggerate the majesty of drapery, and portray themselves in the midst of their families. They also had the leisure to play with their own image, to dress up as a hunter or, as a small unexpected figure, to outline themselves in a back-shop. Their esteem was great enough for them to imprint their shadow on a new canvas engraved with an inscription in gold letters.

◁ Charles Le Brun,
*Charles Le Brun
and Pierre Mignard,
Chief Painters to the King*,
Paris, 17th century.
Oil on canvas, 130 x 140 cm.

◁ Nicolas Poussin,
Portrait of the Artist,
Rome, 1650.
Oil on canvas, 98 x 74 cm.

△ Rembrandt Harmensz van Rijn,
Portrait of the Bareheaded Artist,
Amsterdam, 1633.
Oil on wood, 60 x 47 cm.

◁Left:
François Desportes,
Self-portrait in Hunting Dress, Paris,
1699. Oil on canvas, 197 x 163 cm.

◁Centre:
Gerard Dou, *Self-portrait*,
Leyden, 17th century.
Oil on wood, 31 x 21 cm.

◁Right:
Gerard Dou, *The Village Grocer*
(the painter is on the left,
in the background), Leyden, 1647.
Oil on wood, 38.5 x 29 cm.

◁Left:
Pierre Mignard,
Portrait of the Artist,
Paris, 1690.
Oil on canvas,
235 x 188 cm.

◁Right:
Otto Venius,
*Otto Venius
and His Family*,
Anvers, pre-1629.
Oil on canvas,
176 x 250 cm.

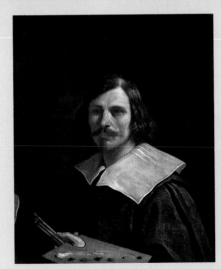

△Giovanni Francesco Barbieri,
known as Guerchin, *Portrait of the Artist
Holding a Palette*, Italy, 17th century.
Oil on canvas, 77 x 62 cm.

△Rembrandt Harmensz van Rijn,
*Portrait of the Artist Wearing
a Cap and a Gold Chain*, Amsterdam,
1633. Oil on wood, 70 x 53 cm.

Antoine Coypel,
Esther Fainting,
Paris, 1704.
Oil on canvas,
105 x 137 cm.

By the death of Louis XIV, France had become an academic country. Societies of artists and scholars, and academies founded by the State defended the professional interests of their members, supporting and regulating production. Created in 1648, the Royal Academy of Painting and Sculpture provided teaching and organised the first public exhibitions. In 1661, it was the turn of the Royal Academy of Dance, followed two years later by the Academy of Inscriptions and Literature. The French Academy in Rome and the Royal Academy of Science were created in 1666. In 1671, the Royal Academy of Music succeeded the Academy of Opera founded in 1669; the Academy of Architecture was also created that same year. Finally, in 1694, the first edition of the *Dictionary of the French Academy* - founded in 1634 - was published. Nearly all of these institutions are still exist today.

Nicolas de Largillière,
Studies of Hands, Paris,
circa 1715. Oil on canvas,
65 x 52 cm.

Jean Jouvenet, *Doctor Raymond Finot*, Paris,
1704. Oil on canvas, 73 x 59 cm.

Antoine Watteau, *The Pilgrimage to the Island of Cythera*, Paris, 1717. Oil on canvas, 129 x 194 cm.

Antoine Watteau, *Gathering in a Park*, Paris, circa 1717-1718. Oil on canvas, 32.5 x 46.5 cm.

COMEDY, PANTOMIME AND DANCE: PARIS ENTERTAINMENT

In order to attract the public, Regency theatres tried to outdo each other in musical entertainment, ballets and monologues. One would adjust one's pirouette, and add the occasional brawl. In 1716, the Italian players returned to the *Hôtel de Bourgogne* in *Les Halles*, the same players who were chased out of Paris in 1697. At the Palais-Royal, the Opera installed its machinery and had the monopoly of operatic entertainment. The French players became established on the Left Bank; and, lastly, the different fairs thrived each season: the Saint-Laurent fair in the spring, and the Saint-Germain fair in the autumn. Italian valets and French farces appeared and disappeared, and the comical effects travelled from one stage to the other. The simpleton dressed in white, with a powdered face, round hat, and a guitar on his back was Pierrot, the former Pedrolino. The adventurer and rogue was Harlequin with his beautiful supernumerary, Harlequina or Columbine. The musician Mezzetin, Scapin, Punchinello, and Scaramouche... were also portrayed.

▷Antoine Watteau,
Pierrot, formerly known as *Gilles*,
Paris, circa 1720. Oil on canvas,
184.5 x 149.5 cm.

◁Left:
Nicolas Lancret,
The Commedia dell'arte Players
or *The Italian Theatre*,
Paris, pre-1743.
Oil on wood,
25.5 x 22 cm.

◁Right:
Claude Gillot,
The Two Carriages,
scene from the comedy
La Foire de Saint-Germain
by Regnard and Dufresny,
Paris, circa 1707.
Oil on canvas,
127 x 160 cm.

△ Above:
Jean-Baptiste Pater,
Gathering of Commedia dell'arte Players in a Park, Paris,
pre-1736. Oil on canvas,
24 x 32 cm.

△ Above left:
Claude Gillot,
The Death of Master André,
scene from the comedy
by Brugière de Barante,
Paris, circa 1710.
Oil on canvas,
100 x 139 cm.

△ Nicolas de Largillière, *Decorative Composition, with Curtains, Landscape and Animals,* Paris, circa 1720-1730. Oil on canvas, 261 x 251 cm.

△ Antoine Watteau,
The Artful Woman,
Paris, circa 1716.
Oil on wood, 25.5 x 19 cm.

△ Antoine Watteau,
The Indifferent Gentleman,
Paris, 1716. Oil on wood,
25.5 x 19 cm.

LOUIS XV DECOR

Carle van Loo, *Halt During the Hunt*, décor of the dining-room
in the King's private apartments at the Château de Fontainebleau,
1737. Oil on canvas, 220 x 250 cm.

Charles Parrocel, *Halt of the Mounted Grenadiers
of the Royal Household*, décor of the dining-room
in the King's private apartments at the Château de Fontainebleau,
1737. Oil on canvas, 219 x 249 cm.

"Rockwork" would henceforth fill interiors, become ornate, and
transform sculptures and furniture. Named "rococo" the following century, this style of rockwork developed a repertoire of shapes taking
their curves from the jagged contours of rocks, their outline from
rocky concretions, and their lines from the patterns of shells. The
painters adapted to this living environment by taking possession of
wainscoting, corner pieces, door frames and dining-room panels.
When the young Louis XV settled at Versailles in 1722, some of the
new apartments were decorated in this style - as were some of the
apartments at Fontainebleau. Hunting, the major royal recreatio-
nal activity, was a recurring theme, even adorning the exotic finery
which inspire dreams of the Orient and call themselves Turkish or
Chinese works of art.

Jean-Baptiste Pater, *Chinese Hunt*, sketch of the décor
for the Petite Galerie of the Château de Versailles, 1736.
Oil on canvas, 55 x 46 cm.

Jean-François de Troy, *Hunting Luncheon*, décor
of the dining-room in the King's private apartments at the Château
de Fontainebleau, 1737. Oil on canvas, 241 x 170 cm.

BOUCHER, SUBLEYRAS

Pierre Subleyras, *The Loving Courtesan*, Rome, circa 1735.
Oil on canvas, 30 x 23 cm.

François Boucher, *Renaud and Armida*, Paris, 1734.
Oil on canvas, 135 x 170 cm.

François Boucher, *The Abduction of Europe*, Paris, 1747.
Oil on canvas, 160 x 193 cm.

By taking his themes from literature and mythology, Boucher conformed to his commissioners' tastes, readily - and artfully - baring all sorts of heroines, whether evolving in his easel paintings, his tapestry sketches, or in his décor for the *Opéra* and *Opéra-Comique*. Armida, the seductive magician, belongs to *The Freed Jerusalem* by Tasse, a poem from 1580. The great Jupiter takes on the form of a white bull to capture Europe, the Phoenician princess. Diana the Huntress is startled by the gaze of Prince Actaeon while bathing - she punishes him by turning him into a stag. Subleyras, who took a *Loving Courtesan* from La Fontaine's *Contes et nouvelles*, had an equally pleasing source of inspiration: "Such beauty so magnificent and proud! Such beauty! I cannot describe it; / To do so, I would need a whole week".

François Boucher, *Diana Bathing,* Paris, 1742. Oil on canvas; 57 x 73 cm.

VARIATIONS ON THE NAKED BODY IN NINE PAINTINGS

Hidden, draped, lewd, revealing, sensual, gallant, free, light, licentious, erotic, academic... An infinite number of terms can be used to describe 18th-century nudes, offering diverse ways of representing the body - usually female: whether blossoming in a pseudo-oriental setting or in antique architectural surroundings; whether claiming to illustrate a legend, or depicting a simple interplay of expressions or a piece of pure painting.

▷François Boucher,
The Odalisque,
Paris, 1745.
Oil on canvas,
53.5 x 64.5 cm.

◁Left:
Antoine Watteau,
Nymph and Satyr,
Paris, circa 1716.
Oil on canvas,
73.5 x 107.5 cm.

◁Right:
Jean Honoré Fragonard,
The Bathers,
Paris, circa 1772-1775.
Oil on canvas,
64 x 80 cm.

◁Left:
Antoine Watteau,
The Judgement of Paris,
Paris, circa 1720.
Oil on wood,
47 x 31 cm.

◁Centre:
Pierre Subleyras,
*Caron Ferrying
the Shadowy Figures*,
Paris, circa 1735-1740.
Oil on canvas,
135 x 83 cm.

◁Right:
Jean-Baptiste Santerre,
Susannah Bathing,
Paris, 1704.
Oil on canvas,
205 x 145 cm.

◁Centre:
Pierre Narcisse Guérin,
*Half-Length Portrait
of a Young Girl*,
Paris, circa 1794.
Oil on canvas,
60.5 x 50 cm.

◁Right:
Marie-Guillemine
Benoist, *Portrait
of an African Woman*,
Paris, 1800.
Oil on canvas,
81 x 65 cm.

◁François Lemoyne,
Hercules and Omphale,
Paris, 1724. Oil on canvas,
184 x 149 cm.

POMPADOUR

Jean-Baptiste Perroneau, *Mme de Sorquainville*, Paris, 1749.
Oil on canvas, 101 x 81 cm.

Jean-Marc Nattier, *Portrait of a Young Woman*, Paris,
1719. Oil on canvas, 74.5 x 60.5 cm.

In the same way as the harpsichord, furniture, books and a globe,
symbols of patronage of the arts and sciences, a woman's clothing
was a sign of her worldly status. To make and create new fashions
was to exercise and consolidate one's strength, and to adorn
oneself in fineries exuding power. By commissioning François
Boucher to paint her portrait, the Marquise de Pompadour, née
Jeanne Antoinette Poisson, clearly intended to mark her status.
The elegant appearance of the ladies of the aristocracy and bourgeoisie, who would place a flower or ribbon at the centre of a low
neckline and arrange their hair in a hairnet, may or may not be
considered to reflect the influence of the professed mistress of
Louis XV.

François Hubert Drouais, *Mme Drouais*, Paris,
circa 1758. Oil on canvas, 82.5 x 62 cm.

François Boucher, *The Marquise de Pompadour (1721-1764)*, Paris, mid-18th century. Oil on paper glued onto canvas, 60 x 45.5 cm.

CHARDIN'S VICTUALS

Jean Siméon Chardin,
The Copper Cistern,
Paris, circa 1734.
Oil on canvas, 28.5 x 23 cm.

Jean Siméon Chardin,
The Skate, Paris, circa 1728.
Oil on canvas, 114 x 146 cm.

Jean Siméon Chardin, *The Silver Goblet*, Paris, circa 1760.
Oil on canvas, 33 x 41 cm.

Jean Siméon Chardin, *Basket of Peaches, with Walnuts, Knife and Glass of Wine*, Paris, 1768. Oil on canvas, 32.5 x 39.5 cm.

Jean Siméon Chardin, *Pipe and Drinking Cup*, known as *The Smoking Room*, Paris, circa 1737. Oil on canvas, 32.5 x 42 cm.

Through devotedly portraying seemingly still lives, Chardin created a laboratory of sorts in which he observed, constructed, arranged and contrasted the objects in the painting. These were the living and the dead, the near and the far, the large and the small, the distinct and the blurred, the rough and the smooth, the goblet seen face on and the diagonally placed knife, the white spot catching the light and the shadow of the jug...

CHARDIN'S FIGURES

The hierarchy of genres continued to reign throughout the 18th century, which vigorously separated the wheat from the chaff. History was on one side, and portraiture and genre painting, on the other. Painters of "saveloys" were right at the bottom. Chardin "produced paintings in various genres for whatever price one was willing to pay. Until about 1737, he had never attempted paintings of figures," wrote Charles Nicolas Cochin in 1780, in his *Essay on the Life of Monsieur Chardin*. "A remarkable occurrence led him to try his hand at this new genre. Monsieur Aved, a portraitist, was a great friend. He often asked Monsieur Chardin, for advice which he found beneficial. However, one day when Monsieur Chardin criticised him too keenly, Monsieur Aved sharply retorted: "Do you suppose that is as easy to paint as your stuffed tongues and saveloys?" Monsieur Chardin was extremely vexed by this remark".

Jean Siméon Chardin, *The Procuress*, Paris, 1739. Oil on canvas, 47 x 38 cm.

Jean Siméon Chardin, *The Industrious Mother*, Paris, 1740. Oil on canvas, 49 x 39 cm.

Jean Siméon Chardin, *The Bird-Organ*, known as *Lady Alternating Her Pastimes*, Paris, 1750-1751. Oil on canvas, 50 x 43 cm.

Jean Siméon Chardin, *Self-portrait at the Easel*, Paris, circa 1776. Pastel on blue paper, 40.7 x 32.5 cm.

"CHILDHOOD SHOULD BE ALLOWED TO REACH MATURITY IN CHILDREN"

Following the example of philosophers, moralists and teachers, painters conveyed images of loving mothers, teatime scenes, and little girls playing with dolls. In 1762, in *Émile or on Education*, Jean-Jacques Rousseau demanded more attention, respect and freedom for children and forbade certain restricting practices such as swaddling or premature weaning. Although a sense of the family was born in the Age of Enlightenment, it appeared to be reserved for the aristocracy and the bourgeoisie. Among the poor, many women still died in childbirth, infanticide was rife, and numerous newborn infants were abandoned - more than seven thousand in Paris alone in 1770. Infants under the age of four had very little chance of survival.

△Jean Siméon Chardin,
Grace, Paris, 1740.
Oil on canvas, 49.5 x 38.5 cm.

◁Left: Anne Geneviève Greuze,
Child with Doll, Paris, pre-1795.
Oil on canvas, 47 x 38 cm.

◁Right: Jean Honoré Fragonard,
Child with Flowers, Paris, circa 1780-1785.
Oil on canvas, 19 x 13 cm.

△ Above: Joshua Reynolds,
Master Hare, London, circa 1788-1789.
Oil on canvas, 77 x 63.5 cm.

△ Above left: François Boucher,
Luncheon, Paris, 1739.
Oil on canvas, 81.5 x 65.5 cm.

△ Above centre: Élisabeth Vigée-Lebrun,
Mme Vigée-Lebrun and Daughter,
Paris, 1789. Oil on wood, 130 x 94 cm.

◁Left: Élisabeth Vigée-Lebrun,
Mme Vigée-Lebrun and Daughter,
Paris, 1786. Oil on wood, 105 x 84 cm.

◁Right: Jacques Louis David,
Mme Pierre Sériziat, Saint-Ouen,
1795. Oil on wood, 131 x 96 cm.

MAGNASCO, TRAVERSI, CRESPI

Alessandro Magnasco, *The Gypsy Meal*, Genoa, circa 1730-1740. Oil on canvas, 80 x 118 cm.

Originating from different regions, three artists bear witness to the mixed reality of 18th-century Italy. Famous in his own lifetime for his sense of the "strange", his brigands, gypsies and fools, sometimes situated in raging nature, Magnasco was admired in Milan, but his art was considered ludicrous on his return to Genoa in 1735. Originally from Naples, Traversi settled in Rome where he composed genre paintings. Crespi, from Bologna, divided his work between religious paintings and picturesque images. Each appearing to be taken from everyday life, and seemingly relating a story, these "scenes from life" nevertheless reflected different narrative modes, the often symbolic significance of which has now been lost.

Gaspare Traversi, *The Brawl*, Rome, circa 1754.
Oil on canvas, 95.5 x 130.5 cm.

Giuseppe Maria Crespi, *The Flea*, Bologna, circa 1720-1725. Oil on canvas, 54 x 40 cm.

ANCIENT AND MODERN ROME

Pompeo Batoni, *Apollo, Music and Measure* (?) ,
Rome, circa 1741. Oil on canvas, 121 x 90 cm.

Giuseppe Antonio Petrini, *The Sleeping Saint Peter* (?),
Lombardy, circa 1730. Oil on canvas, 85 x 115 cm.

Giuseppe Bazzani, *The Daughter of Jephthah*,
Mantua, pre-1769. Oil on canvas, 180 x 233 cm.

Francesco Solimena, *Heliodorus Driven out from the Temple*,
Naples, circa 1723-1725. Oil on canvas, 150 x 200 cm.

Giovanni Paolo Pannini, *Gallery of Views over Modern Rome,* Rome, 1759. Oil on canvas, 231 x 303 cm.

Never before had Rome such passion for antiquity, triumphant architecture and settings. The discovery followed by the archaeological
excavations of Herculanum and Pompeii encouraged a resolutely
new perception of the creations of the ancients. Hence, restora-
tions, copies and collections multiplied: the Museum of Capitole was
founded in 1733; in 1755, Johann Joachim Winckelmann published
his *Reflections on the Imitation of Greek Masterpieces in Painting
and Sculpture,* followed in 1764 by the *History of Ancient Art;* in
1772, the galleries of the Vatican were opened to the public. Ancient
and modern Rome were united by the same ideal, an ideal which
attracted artists, scholars and collectors throughout Europe. Pannini
joined in this celebration while the painters from Lombardy and
elsewhere went in search of other pursuits.

VENETIAN MASTERS

The Venice of the merchants and politicians was on the decline but that of the painters continued to flourish, from the Tiepolo, father and son, to the numerous landscape artists devoted to *veduta*, to the "point at which the view falls", who put places and ceremonies into perspective. Carlo Goldoni's Venice is undoubtedly the most beautiful, as shown in his *Memoirs* of 1787. "Venice is such an extraordinary city that it is impossible to have an accurate image of it without having seen it. Maps, plans, models and descriptions are not enough, one has to see it with one's own eyes. All of the cities in the world resemble each other to a varying degree: but this city is like no other."

Giandomenico Tiepolo,
Christ and the Adulteress, Venice,
1751. Oil on canvas, 84 x 105 cm.

Sebastiano Ricci, *Nymph and Satyrs*, Venice, circa 1712-1716.
Oil on canvas, 64 x 75.5 cm.

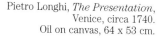

Pietro Longhi, *The Presentation*,
Venice, circa 1740.
Oil on canvas, 64 x 53 cm.

18th CENTURY

Giovanni Antonio Canaletto, *Rialto Bridge*, Venice, circa 1760-1770. Oil on canvas, 119 x 154 cm.

Francesco Guardi, *The Departure of the Bucentaur for the Venice Lido, on Ascension Day*, Venice, 1766-1770. Oil on canvas, 66 x 101 cm.

Joseph Vernet, *Entry to the Port of Marseille*, Marseille, 1754. Oil on canvas, 165 x 263 cm.

Pierre Henri de Valenciennes, *In Rome, Study of an Overcast Sky*, Rome, circa 1780.
Oil on paper glued onto canvas, 23.8 x 38.8 cm.

The flavour of the era, the second half of the 18th century, was caught between an idealised landscape, a picturesque vision and unaffected nature. Joseph Vernet, who spent twenty years or so in Italy, composed the panoramic portrait of twenty-two French ports at the request of the Superintendent of Royal Buildings. Far from any such commission, Valenciennes allowed his cloudy skies invade his studies; Hubert Robert was drawn to the rediscovered antiquity, the strength of a renewed aesthetic quality, that of the true or false ruin, and contemplation of the past as of death.

Hubert Robert, *The Pont de Gard*, commissioned for the Château de Fontainebleau, 1786. Oil on canvas, 242 x 242 cm.

FRAGONARD'S GAZE

Jean Honoré Fragonard, *The Bolt*, Paris, circa 1778. Oil on canvas, 73 x 93 cm.

While Fragonard's scenes are vibrant and voluptuous, in the image of his colour and brushstroke, they are also striking as a result of the painter's technique and subtle mischievousness. A young man stands on tiptoe to reach the bolt in order to detain his loved one, while three-quarters of the painting overflow with the passionate movement of pillows, draperies, and reds. A woman takes off her chemise which stands out against the pearlised greys and whites. Two young ladies, slightly concealed and a little curious, throw flower petals at their onlookers, allowing us to glimpse the pink and red of a breast almost hidden in the painting.

Jean Honoré Fragonard,
Woman Taking off Her Chemise, Paris, pre-1778.
Oil on canvas, 35 x 42.5 cm.

Jean Honoré Fragonard, *The Curious Young Ladies*, Paris, circa 1767-1771. Oil on wood, 16.5 x 12.5 cm.

FRAGONARD'S FANCIES

Not sitting quite where one would expect, evading all categorisation in order to achieve one's freedom: this may have been one of Fragonard's approaches. His *"figures de fantaisie"*, or fanciful figures, in fact bring together all of the different genres: studies of a gesture and the bearing of a head; portraits of friends and commissioners, a writer or singer; figures in theatrical costumes, sporting a 17th-century ruff or a feathered hat; a display of virtuosity, presence and speed; allegories of Music and Inspiration; paintings constituting a private "portrait gallery"; or easel paintings derived from a sketch... These figures clearly combine every genre but conform to none.

Jean Honoré Fragonard,
Inspiration, Paris, circa 1769.
Oil on canvas, 80.5 x 64.5 cm.

Jean Honoré Fragonard, *Music*, Paris, 1769.
Oil on canvas, 80 x 65 cm.

Jean Honoré Fragonard, *Study*, also known as *The Song*,
Paris, circa 1769. Oil on canvas, 81.5 x 65.5 cm.

Jean Honoré Fragonard, *Fanciful Figure*, Paris, circa 1769. Oil on canvas, 80 x 65 cm.

"AT THE SIGHT OF THE PAINTINGS EXHIBITED THIS YEAR AT THE SALON..."

"I finally caught sight of it, the painting by our friend Greuze; but not without difficulty; it is still drawing a crowd. It is *A Father Who Has Just Paid His Daughter's Dowry*. It is a moving subject, and it slightly stirs one to look at it. I found the composition extremely beautiful; that is exactly how it ought to have happened". In front of *The Village Sweetheart* by Greuze, the highlight of the *Salon* of 1761, Diderot could barely suppress his enthusiasm. Through his reviews of the *Salons* from 1759 to 1781, the philosopher and supporter of Fragonard, Chardin and Vernet became an art critic, commenting on the painting exhibitions which had been held at the Louvre for a century - since they were first organised by Colbert in 1667. On 10 August 1793, the *Salon Carré* and *Grande Galerie* of the Louvre were to be the setting for a revolutionary museum, the *Muséum Central des Arts*.

◁ Louis Michel Van Loo,
Denis Diderot,
Paris, Salon of 1767.
Oil on canvas, 81 x 65 cm.

◁ Jean-Jacques Lagrenée,
the Younger, *Allegory Relating to the Creation of the Museum*,
Paris, 1793. Oil on canvas.

△ Top left: Jean-Baptiste Greuze,
The Village Sweetheart, Paris, *Salon* of 1761.
Oil on canvas, 92 x 117 cm.

△ Top centre: Jean-Baptiste Greuze,
The Punished Son, Paris, 1778.
Oil on canvas, 130 x 163 cm.

△ Top right: Jean-Baptiste Greuze,
Self-portrait, Paris, circa 1769.
Oil on canvas, 73 x 59 cm.

◁ Left: Gabriel de Saint-Aubin,
View of the Salon du Louvre in 1779,
Paris, 1779. Oil on paper glued onto canvas,
19.3 x 44 cm.

△ Hubert Robert, *Development Project for the Mars
Rotunda at the Louvre*, Paris, circa 1797-1800.
Oil on canvas glued onto cardboard, 41 x 54 cm.

△ Hubert Robert, *Development Project for the Grande Galerie
of the Louvre in 1796*, Paris, 1796. Oil on canvas, 46 x 55 cm.
Hubert Robert is painting on the right.

DAVID THE REVOLUTIONARY

Jacques Louis David, *The Rape of the Sabine Women*, Paris, 1799. Oil on canvas, 385 x 522 cm.

What was the role of a citizen artist in 1789? How could one serve both the Revolution and the patriotic ideal, and how could one depict bravery and heroism? Jacques Louis David chose to join the political struggle and go into battle in his art: the return to the Antique and the depiction of sacrifice. Having become a Deputy of the Convention and seated among the Montagnards, the painter voted for the death of the king, belonged to the General Security Committee and the State Education Committee, became the organiser of festivities held in honour of the Republican armies or in honour of the Supreme Being, and supported and then fell with Robespierre. Incarcerated in 1794, David returned under the *Directoire*.

Pierre Narcisse Guérin,
The Return of Marcus Sextus,
Paris, 1799. Oil on canvas,
217 x 243 cm.

Jacques Louis David, *The Oath of the Horatii*, Paris, 1785. Oil on canvas, 330 x 425 cm.

GÉRARD, PRUD'HON, GIRODET

François Gérard, *Psyche and Cupid*, Paris, 1798.
Oil on canvas, 186 x 132 cm.

Anne Louis Girodet de Roucy-Trioson, *Endymion, Moonlight Effect*,
known as *The Sleep of Endymion*, Paris, 1792. Oil on canvas, 198 x 261 cm.

Pierre Paul Prud'hon,
*Justice and Divine
Vengeance Pursuing Crime*,
Paris, 1808. Oil on canvas,
244 x 294 cm.

Anne Louis Girodet de Roucy-Trioson, *Atala in the Tomb*, Paris, 1808. Oil on canvas, 207 x 267 cm.

From the end of the 18th century to the beginning of the 19th century, history swung from the storming of the Bastille to the reign of an emperor. Neoclassicism, pre-Romanticism and Romanticism existed alongside each other from the 1790s to approximately 1810. In 1792, Girodet bathed the beautiful Endymion, who was loved by the Moon (Selene), in pearly light, and the First Republic was declared on the 21st of September, the beginning of the year I. In 1793, the painting was shown at the *Salon*. Louis XVI was guillotined on the 21st of January that same year. In 1798, Gérard painted the portrait of Psyche and Cupid. On the 18th of Brumaire in the year VIII (9th of November 1799), Bonaparte's *coup d'état* brought an end to the *Directoire*. In 1808, *Atala in the Tomb* was inspired by Chateaubriand, and an allegory was composed by Prud'hon; France was at the height of the Napoleonic Wars and Spain surrendered on the 5th of May.

A MONKEY, A MOCKER AND A MODEL: ALLEGORIES OF PAINTING

Presenting his own activity, defining his place in the creation of a painting was one of the delightful techniques sometimes used by the artist in *mises en abyme* and modern allegories. He mockingly points to the onlooker contemplating his work. He philosophically depicts an animal which, in front of the easel, imitates the artist who "apes" nature or simply mimics someone who is nothing more than a mere imitator... He respectfully relates ancient legends which prevail in the practice of his art when painting attempted to emulate the beauty of women. As an observer, he paints the portrait of apprentice draughtsmen or of the more lowly who pose for him.

◁ Joseph Ducreux,
Portrait of the Artist as a Mocker,
Paris, circa 1791.
Oil on canvas,
91.5 x 72.5 cm.

▽ Gaspare Traversi,
The Sitting,
Rome, 1754.
Oil on canvas,
99 x 130 cm.

△ Jean Siméon Chardin,
The Painting Monkey, Paris, 1740.
Oil on canvas, 73 x 59.5 cm.

◁ François André Vincent,
*Zeuxis Choosing His Models
from the Most Beautiful
Daughters of Crotona,*
Paris, 1789. Oil on canvas,
323 x 415 cm.

◁Left:
Anne Vallayer-Coster,
*The Attributes of Painting,
Sculpture and Architecture,*
Paris, 1769. Oil on canvas,
90 x 121 cm.

△Right:
François André Vincent,
*Portrait of Three Men
(the Artist, Rousseau
the Architect,
and an Unknown Person),*
Marseille, 1775.
Oil on canvas, 81 x 98 cm.

△Jean Siméon Chardin,
*Young Draughtsman
Sharpening His Pencil,*
Paris, 1737. Oil on canvas,
80 x 65 cm.

△Nicolas Bernard Lépicié,
The Young Draughtsman,
Paris, 1772. Oil on canvas,
41 x 33 cm.

△Jean-Baptiste Greuze,
*Joseph, Model from the Royal
Academy Holding a Frying Pan,*
Paris, 1755. Oil on canvas,
68 x 58 cm.

DIRECTOIRE AND CONSULATE

Artists at the end of the 18th century, the Age of Enlightenment and Reason, sought notoriety, self-confident and certain of the validity of their task, and aware of their role in a society in which they embraced both moral and aesthetic high values. Displaying fine *Directoire* elegance, a shade eccentric, posing in a studio where the prevailing themes were Minerva and allegories of the Arts, the artists were gentlemen and moved in the best circles, a world frequented by scholars, writers and thinkers who conversed in the literary salons – such as that held by Mme Récamier.

François Gérard,
The Painter Isabey and His Daughter Alexandrine,
Paris, 1795. Oil on canvas, 194 x 130 cm.

Louis Léopold Boilly,
Gathering of Artists in Isabey's Studio,
Paris, 1798. Oil on canvas, 71.5 x 111 cm.

Jacques Louis David, *Mme Récamier*, Paris, unfinished painting begun in 1800. Oil on canvas, 174 x 244 cm.

Anne Louis Girodet de Roucy-Trioson,
The Young Romainville Trioson,
Paris, 1800. Oil on canvas, 73 x 59 cm.

BRITAIN

Ranking among the most fashionable British portraitists, and chairman of the newly founded Royal Academy in London in 1768, Sir Joshua Reynolds based artistic perfection on a genuine understanding of nature. To appreciate this, let us remember "what our anatomy professor taught us about natural posture and the movement of the feet," he stated in a *Discourse on Painting* in 1770. "He observed that the manner of turning them outwards was contrary to nature's intentions, as may be seen in the bone structure and the weakness resulting from this type of posture. We can also include the habit of holding one's head straight, sticking out one's chest, walking with one's knees braced, and several other actions which we know to be the result of fashion, which nature never intended".

Henry Raeburn, *Young Girl Holding Flowers*, known as *Innocence: Portrait of Nancy Graham*, Edinburgh, 1798-1800. Oil on canvas, 91 x 71 cm.

Thomas Lawrence, *The Children of John Angerstein*, London, 1808. Oil on canvas, 194 x 144 cm.

Johann Heinrich Füssli, *Lady Macbeth*, London, 1784. Oil on canvas, 221 x 160 cm.

Thomas Gainsborough, *Lady Alston*, London, circa 1760-1765. Oil on canvas, 226 x 168 cm.

THE PORTRAIT
AND THE LANDSCAPE,
THE SOUL AND ITS REFLECTION

"A few days ago, I was in the countryside at the house of a friend: numerous ladies and horsemen had gathered there. One morning I took it into my head to go for walk alone in the wood on the estate: I had already disappeared into the darkest paths when the rain took me by surprise; I ran towards an arbour that I saw before me to take shelter. I was about to step inside when I head voices: I stopped to listen; it was two ladies from our gathering who had apparently taken refuge there before me." In 1719, Marivaux' nature was made up of arbours and small shelters. Sometimes domesticated, sometimes rustic, filled with antique-style follies, woods and streams, the 18th-century landscape was evocative of mood. Conversation, happiness, and lovers' games found refuge there, as did solitude and sadness.

△ Thomas Gainsborough,
Conversation in a Park,
London, circa 1746-1747.
Oil on canvas, 73 x 68 cm.

◁ Left:
Jacques de Lajoue,
The Artist's Family,
Paris, 1737. Oil on canvas,
124 x 97 cm.

◁ Right:
Antoine Watteau,
Portrait of a Gentleman,
Paris, circa 1715-1720.
Oil on canvas, 130 x 97 cm.

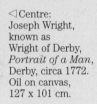

MELÉNDEZ, GOYA

One devoted himself to culinary objects and fruits in particular, and the other to the human figure. Both represent more than half a century of Spanish painting. Having settled in Madrid in 1755, Meléndez offered Charles III in 1773 "a collection of forty-four paintings, with every delicacy that the Spanish climate had to offer, produced with the help of the four elements and the four seasons, while he himself does not have the means to feed himself, having no other inheritance than his brushes". In 1786, Goya became painter to the King. Sometimes dazzling monochromes, his portraits would be innumerable.

Francisco Goya y Lucientes,
Ferdinand Guillemardet,
Madrid, 1798. Oil on canvas,
186 x 124 cm.

Luis Meléndez, *Portrait of the Artist Holding a Nude*, Paris (?), 1746.
Oil on canvas, 99.5 x 82 cm.

Francisco Goya y Lucientes,
Lady with a Fan,
Madrid, circa 1805-1810.
Oil on canvas, 103 x 83 cm.

Francisco Goya y Lucientes, *Countess del Carpio, Marquise of La Solana*, Madrid, circa 1793.
Oil on canvas, 181 x 122 cm.

BONAPARTE

Antoine Jean Gros, *Bonaparte Visiting the Plague-Stricken of Jaffa, 11 March 1799*, Paris, *Salon* of 1804. Oil on canvas, 523 x 715 cm.

"What a beautiful face he has! So pure, so great, as beautiful as the ancients! [...] This is a man who would have been worshipped in Antiquity [...]. Bonaparte is my hero." After his first meeting with the former commander-in-chief of the interior army in approximately 1797, David, fascinated and instantly won over, transformed the military hero into a painted hero. General, First Consul and then Consul for life, Napoleon Bonaparte succeeded in bringing together the former classicists and the future romanticists in the same beliefs: Gros and his master, David, followed him into the new century, the beginning of the 19th century that would see the crowning of an emperor.

Jacques Louis David,
The General Bonaparte,
sketch of a painting
which was to show
Bonaparte looking at the Alps,
Paris, circa 1797-1798.
Oil on canvas, 81 x 65 cm.

Antoine Jean Gros, *Bonaparte on the Bridge of Arcole, 17 November 1796*, sketch of the painting in the National Museum of the Château de Versailles, Genoa, 1796. Oil on canvas, 73 x 59 cm.

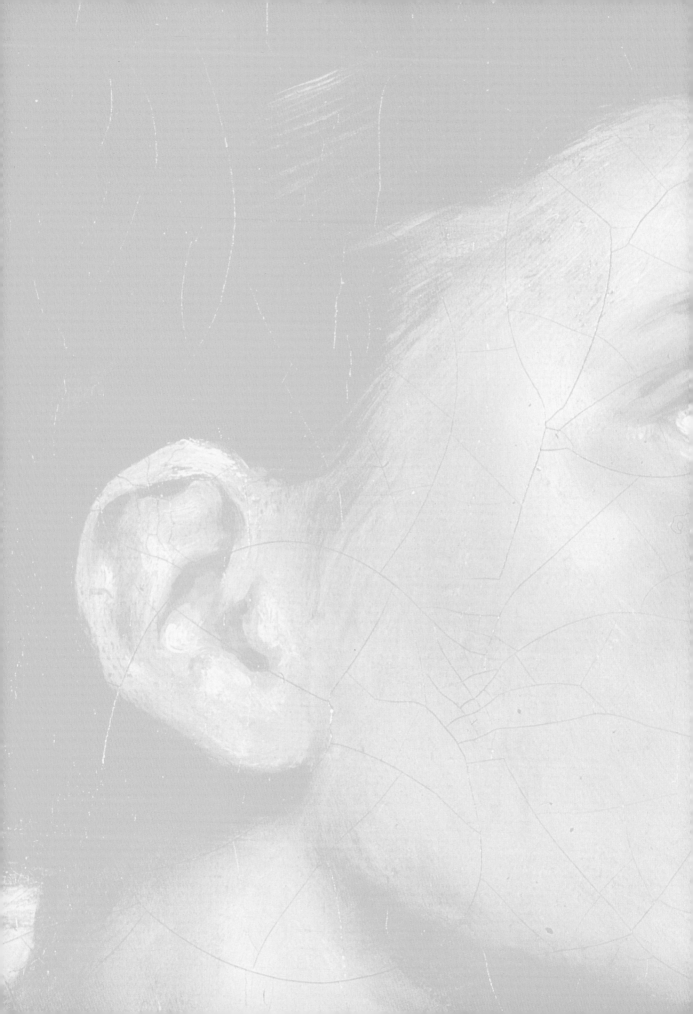

19th CENTURY

THE FIRST EMPIRE

Jacques Louis David, *The Coronation of Emperor Napoleon I and the Crowning of Empress Josephine in the Notre-Dame Cathedral in Paris, 2 December 1804*, Paris, 1806-1807. Oil on canvas, 621 x 979 cm.

A fine strategist, Napoleon I was unsurpassed in the fabrication of his legend. Armed with censorship in order to control the press and stifle literature, he spread propaganda and distributed a new catechism to children. The *Bulletins* of the *Grande Armée* were displayed on posters, peddled, read in theatres and translated into several languages, re-living the battles, occasionally overlooking a few errors, adjusting certain figures and lowering the number of deaths - "to lie like a bulletin" became a common French expression. It fell to art and Napoleon's painter, David, to elaborate the image of an emperor, surrounded by his people, consecrated "by the grace of God and the Institutions of the Republic", and who alone was able to crown his empress.

Jacques Louis David,
Portrait of the Artist,
Paris, 1794. Oil on canvas,
81 x 64 cm.

249

THE NAPOLEONIC WARS

On the 8th of February 1807, in East Prussia, the Russians were defeated by the armies of Napoleon I. However, the outcome of the Battle of Eylau is still uncertain, and France's losses too great. Situated the day after the battle, the striking painting commissioned from Gros portrays the humanity and clemency of the Emperor comforting his troops and demanding aid for the wounded enemy. Initiated in June 1812, the Russian campaign ended with a disastrous and deadly retreat: of the seven hundred thousand men enlisted, only thirty thousand would return - leaving one hundred thousand prisoners and four hundred thousand dead. Napoleon I abdicated on the 4th of April 1814.

Antoine Jean Gros, *Napoleon on the Battlefield of Eylau, 9 February 1807*, Paris, 1808. Oil on canvas, 521 x 784 cm.

Théodore Géricault, *Officer of the Cavalry of the Imperial Guard Charging*, Paris, 1812. Oil on canvas, 349 x 266 cm.

Antoine Jean Gros, *Joachim Murat, King of Naples*, Paris, 1812. Oil on canvas, 343 x 280 cm.

Théodore Géricault, *Wounded Armoured Cavalryman Leaving the Battlefield*, Paris, 1814. Oil on canvas, 358 x 294 cm.

PORTRAITS OF THE BOURGEOISIE

Jean Auguste Dominique Ingres, *Louis François Bertin*, founder of the *Journal des débats*, Paris, 1832. Oil on canvas, 116 x 95 cm.

Jean Auguste Dominique Ingres, *Mme Rivière*, wife of Philibert Rivière, man of business, Paris, 1806. Oil on canvas, 116 x 90 cm.

Marguerite Gérard, *The Bad News*, Paris, 1804. Oil on canvas, 63.5 x 50.5 cm.

The *Salons* of the 19th century abounded in portraits, an almost vital source of income for Parisian artists. In 1834, six hundred and fifty modern effigies were presented to the public, the majority of which marked the triumph of new commissioners, originating from the bourgeoisie. It was these models posing in the dress and interiors of their time which so irritated Théophile Gautier in his review of 1837. "It would be impossible to imagine anything more unsightly, more pathetic, or more shabby than the clothes that we are obliged to wear and that the painters, who give themselves over to this disagreeable occupation of portraying us in duplicate, are forced to copy with such accuracy: we are not inordinately beautiful, but we could most certainly be less ghastly."

Jean Auguste Dominique Ingres, *Mlle Caroline Rivière*, Paris, 1806. Oil on canvas, 100 x 70 cm.

THE ARTISTS OF THE PAST
HAVE BECOME
THE HEROES OF TODAY

The artists of the Renaissance and the 17th century now belong to the pantheon of the Great. Next to Homer they mingle with poets, princes pay them rightful homage, and they work elegantly in a fashionable studio. By retelling and rewriting the history of their ancestors, artists placed themselves under the patronage of tutelary genius, and asserted the nobleness of their task. By claiming the image of their forefathers, 19th-century artists, often marked by a tragic destiny, in turn became heroic.

▷ Jean Auguste Dominique Ingres, *Homer Deified*, known as *The Apotheosis of Homer* (Nicolas Poussin is shown at the bottom left of the painting), Paris, 1827. Oil on canvas, 386 x 512 cm. Former ceiling of the Clarac Room in the Egyptian antiquities section of the Louvre (replaced by a copy).

◁Left:
Horace Vernet,
*Raphael in the
Vatican*, Rome, 1832.
Oil on canvas,
392 x 300 cm.

◁Right:
Alexandre Hesse,
*Final Tribute to Titian,
Who Died in Venice
During the Plague
of 1576*, Paris, 1833.
Oil on canvas,
163 x 233 cm.

◁Left:
François Marius Granet,
*Sodoma the Painter
Taken to Hospital*, Rome, 1815.
Oil on canvas, 75 x 100 cm.

◁Right:
Alexandre Évariste Fragonard,
*François I Receiving
the Paintings Brought Back
from Italy by Primaticcio*,
Paris, 1830. Oil on plaster block,
22.5 x 22.5 cm.
Sketch for the ceiling
of the Charles X Museum
at the Louvre
(transferred to room 39)

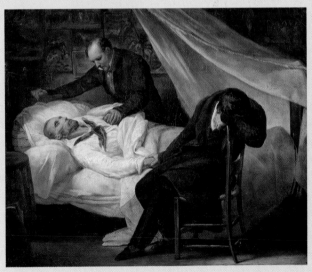

△ Ferdinand De Braekeleer, *Rubens Painting "The Straw Hat"*,
Anvers, 1826. Oil on canvas, 100 x 123 cm.

△ Ary Scheffer, *The Death of Géricault, 26 January 1824*,
Paris, 1824. Oil on canvas, 36 x 46 cm.

INGRES, FLANDRIN

Considered a superior form, a sign of purity or universality, drawing found its legitimacy in one of the essential myths of art in relation to colour which for some served to depict emotion or even food. This was what Ingres and his pupil, Flandrin, stood for and emphasised. According to the ancient legend handed down by Pliny the Elder and changing over the eras, the daughter of a Corinthian potter cherished a young man who was about to set out on a long journey. By the light of a torch she marked the contour of his profile on a wall: since she could not keep her lover, she kept the outline of his shadow. Painting was then able to be born from these very first lines.

Hippolyte Flandrin, *Naked Young Man Sitting by the Sea. Study Figure*, Rome, 1836. Oil on canvas, 98 x 124 cm.

Jean Auguste Dominique Ingres, *Oedipus Explaining the Enigma of the Sphinx*, Rome, 1808. Oil on canvas, 189 x 144 cm.

Jean Auguste Dominique Ingres, *An Odalisque*, known as *The Large Odalisque*, Rome, 1814. Oil on canvas, 91 x 162 cm.

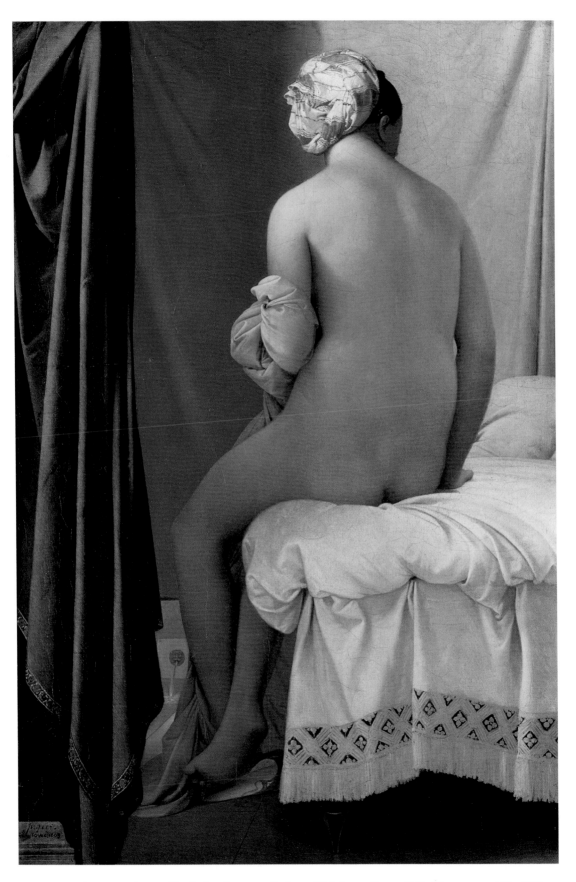

Jean Auguste Dominique Ingres, *The Bather*, known as *Bather of Valpinçon*, Rome, 1808. Oil on canvas, 146 x 97.5 cm.

257

GERICAULT'S SHIPWRECKS

Théodore Géricault, *The Tempest* or *The Wreck*, Paris, circa 1812-1816. Oil on canvas, 19 x 25 cm.

Théodore Géricault, *Scene of the Flood*, Paris, circa 1818-1820. Oil on canvas, 97 x 130 cm.

Théodore Géricault, *The Raft of the Medusa*, Paris, 1819. Oil on canvas, 491 x 716 cm.

Théodore Géricault ceaselessly observed his contemporary surroundings, transcribing the effects of the sky and sea, isolating fragments of the body. In his Parisian studio situated on *rue des Martyrs*, then *rue du Faubourg-du-Roule*, he composed small paintings of human limbs, having access to dissected corpses at the Hôpital Beaujon. His studies take on diversified forms, often inspired by contemporary events: boxers - who then fought with bare fists, the slave trade, the faces of lunatics, and the fifteen survivors of the shipwrecked *Medusa* in 1816.

Théodore Géricault, *Study of the Arm and Hand*, Paris, 1819. Oil on canvas, 18 x 33.5 cm.

GERICAULT'S PASSION

Théodore Géricault, *The Horse Race*, known as *The Epsom Derby*, England, 1821. Oil on canvas, 92 x 122 cm.

Théodore Géricault, *The Plaster Kiln*, Paris,
circa 1821-1822. Oil on canvas, 50 x 61 cm.

"A few days ago, I spent the evening with Géricault," wrote
Eugène Delacroix, seven years his junior, in his *Journal* on
Tuesday the 30th of December 1823. "I sincerely pray he will live,
but I have lost hope. What a terrible change! I remember that I
came away completely enraptured by his painting: *particularly
a study of the face of a cavalryman*. I must never be forgotten.
It is a milestone. The beautiful studies! What assurance! What
superiority! And to die next to this, work which one created in the
strength and ardour of youth, when one can no longer move an
inch on one's bed without the help of others !" Passionate about
horses, whether racehorses or battle horses, Géricault died on the
26th of January 1824, at the age of thirty-two. That same year,
Delacroix would have much to say about him.

Théodore Géricault, *Wild Horse Race in Rome,* study, Rome, circa 1817.
Oil on paper glued onto canvas, 45 x 60 cm.

Théodore Géricault, *Horse Attacked by a Lion*, Paris, pre-1824. Oil on canvas, 54 x 65 cm.

DELACROIX' MANIFESTOS

At the *Salon* of 1824, the very sight of the *Scenes of the Massacres of Scio* seemed intolerable. Was this because of its terrible topicality, the cause defended in the painting - Greece's war of independence, then under Turkish domination? Was the artist taking a stand? Was it a fight in the battle of romanticism? If it was indeed a massacre, it was surely a "massacre of painting", wrote Étienne Jean Delécluze, a pupil of David. At the *Salon* of 1827, the whole thing started again and the portrayal of another massacre caused a scandal. Delécluze persisted, and "the intelligence of the onlooker was unable to make its way into a subject in which every detail is isolated, where the eye cannot unravel the confused lines and colours, and where the primary rules of art appear to have been ignored by prejudice. *Sardanapalus* is a painter's mistake". Freeing pieces of colour, blurring and swinging the planes, sowing confusion in order to disrupt the vision: such was the path chosen by Delacroix.

Eugène Delacroix, *Scenes of the Massacres of Scio, Greek Families Awaiting Death or Slavery*, Paris, 1824. Oil on canvas, 419 x 354 cm.

Eugène Delacroix, *Lion and Boar*, Paris, 1853. Oil on canvas, 46.5 x 56.5 cm.

Eugène Delacroix, *Young Orphan at the Cemetery*, Paris, 1824. Oil on canvas, 65.5 x 54.5 cm.

Eugène Delacroix, *The Death of Sardanapalus*, Paris, 1827. Oil on canvas, 392 x 496 cm.

KEEPING WATCH,
POSSESSING, FLAUNTING, TORTURING…
EXERCICES IN CRUELTY

"A well-drawn figure fills you with pleasure totally unrelated to the subject. Voluptuous or terrible, this figure owes its charm solely to the sinuous lines that it makes in space. If skilfully drawn, the limbs of a flayed martyr and the body of a swooning nymph evoke a certain type of pleasure in the elements having nothing whatsoever to do with the subject; if you find otherwise, I can only assume that you are either a torturer or a libertine."

Charles Baudelaire,
The Life and Work of Delacroix, 1863.

△ Eugène Delacroix, *The Enraged Medea*, Paris, 1862.
Oil on canvas, 122 x 84.5 cm.

◁Left:
Eugène Delacroix,
*Study of a Female
Nude Lying
on a Divan*, known as
*The Woman with
White Stockings*,
Paris, circa 1830.
Oil on canvas,
26 x 33 cm.

◁Right:
William Etty,
*Female Nude
From Behind*, London,
circa 1835-1840.
Oil on cardboard,
66.5 x 50.5 cm.

◁Left:
Théodore Chassériau,
*Andromeda
Fastened to the Rock
by the Nereids*,
Paris, 1840.
Oil on canvas,
92 x 74 cm.

◁Right:
Théodore Chassériau,
*The Abandoned
Ariadne*, Paris,
circa 1850.
Oil on canvas,
20.5 x 32 cm.

◁Left:
Jean Auguste
Dominique Ingres,
*Roger Releasing
Angelica*, Rome,
1819. Oil on canvas,
147 x 190 cm.

◁Right:
Paul Delaroche,
The Young Martyr,
Paris, 1855.
Oil on canvas,
170.5 x 148 cm.

CHASSÉRIAU

Edgar Degas was fascinated by Ingres' line and admired the fluid lines of Chassériau's bodies and also his portraits, even though the studies of the artist who painted dancers would take on a different form, because "until now," he stated, "the nude has always been depicted in poses that would suggest an audience. However, my women are simple people [...]. I portray them without affectation, as animals grooming themselves." The pose of Esther, the Jewish heroine ready to receive every tribute, and that of Daphne, the untouchable nymph adored by a deity and who was turned into a laurel-bush at Apollo's touch, both imply the gaze of an audience.

Théodore Chassériau,
Apollo and Daphne, Paris, 1846.
Oil on canvas, 53 x 35.5 cm.

Théodore Chassériau, *Portrait of the Artist Holding a Palette*, Paris, 1838. Oil on canvas, 73 x 59.5 cm.

Théodore Chassériau, *The Two Sisters*, Paris, 1843.
Oil on canvas, 99 x 82 cm.

Théodore Chassériau, *Esther Preparing Herself to Be Presented to King Ahasuerus*, known as *Esther at Her Toilet*, Paris, 1841.
Oil on canvas, 45.5 x 35.5 cm.

DELACROIX' SUBJECTS

Eugène Delacroix, *Portrait of the Artist*,
Paris, circa 1837. Oil on canvas,
65 x 54.5 cm.

Eugène Delacroix, *Dante and Virgil*, known as *Dante's Boat*, Paris, 1822.
Oil on canvas, 189 x 241 cm.

Sketching out definitions for a dictionary
on fine art, Delacroix attacked the vocabulary of art. Contour, line and shadow.
"There is no such thing as actual shadows.
There are only reflections" and "each
reflection has some of the characteristics
of green, and the edges of the shadow,
purple". Dust, liaison, vagueness and foreshortening. The brushstroke "employed
as is proper serves more appropriately to
express the different planes of the objects.
Highly accentuated, it brings them for-
ward: the opposite causes them to retreat".
The subject, ancient or contemporary.
"Importance of the subject. Subjects taken
from legend always original. Modern subjects difficult to handle in the absence of
the nude and due to the poorness of the
costumes. The originality of the painter
does not always require a subject"
(*Journal*, January 1857).

Eugène Delacroix, *The Capture of Constantinople by the Crusaders, 12 April 1204*,
Paris, 1840. Oil on canvas, 411 x 497 cm.

Eugène Delacroix, *28 July 1830: Liberty Guiding the People*, Paris, 1830. Oil on canvas, 260 x 325 cm.

THE PICTURESQUE,
LIGHT AND THE FEMALE BODY:
ORIENTAL FIGURES

Each era creates its own Orient. The changing Orient of the 19th century conjured up images of harems and voluptuous odalisques, recreated inaccessible feminine intimacy in the studio, or observed a musician and dancers in Mogador. Filled with curiosity, many painters went in search of light, the exotic, and another world. In July 1830, French troops seized Algiers. The colonised Orient offered itself up, within arm's reach.

△ Théodore Chassériau,
Woman Bathing in a Harem,
Paris, 1849. Oil on canvas,
50 x 32 cm.

△ Eugène Delacroix, *Women of Algiers
in Their Apartment*, Paris, 1834.
Oil on canvas, 180 x 229 cm.

△ Top: Jean Auguste Dominique Ingres,
The Turkish Bath, Paris, 1862. Oil on canvas, d: 108 cm.

◁Left: Eugène Delacroix,
Jewish Musicians of Mogador, Paris,
1847. Oil on canvas, 46 x 55.5 cm.

◁Right:
Alexandre Gabriel Decamps,
Fording the River, Paris, 1853.
Oil on canvas, 58.5 x 118 cm.

◁Left:
Eugène Delacroix,
*Turk Smoking,
Sitting on a Divan*,
Paris, 1825.
Oil on canvas,
25 x 30 cm.

◁Right:
Eugène Fromentin,
Moorish Burial,
Paris, 1853.
Oil on canvas,
32.5 x 56 cm.

△Above:
Eugène Delacroix,
Jewish Wedding in Morocco,
Paris, 1839. Oil on canvas,
105 x 140 cm.

△Above left:
Eugène Delacroix, *Odalisque*,
Paris, circa 1848-1849.
Oil on canvas, 24 x 32.5 cm.

△Above centre:
Théodore Chassériau,
*Moroccan Dancers.
The Dance with Scarves*,
Paris, 1849. Oil on canvas,
32 x 40 cm.

△Alexandre Gabriel Decamps,
Leaving the Turkish School, Paris, circa 1850.
Oil on canvas, 66 x 89.5 cm.

△François Marius Granet, *Ransom
of Prisoners in the Prisons of Algiers*,
Paris, 1831. Oil on canvas, 151 x 200 cm.

Carl Spitzweg, *Reading the Bible, in the Evening*, Munich, circa 1845-1850. Oil on wood, 29.5 x 23 cm.

Caspar David Friedrich, *Tree with Crows*, Germany, circa 1822. Oil on canvas, 59 x 74 cm.

Having left to study in Copenhagen where he learned three types of drawing - freehand, copying from classical moulds and drawing from nature, Friedrich developed a remarkable landscape art in Dresden, making note of, enhancing and combining each element taken from nature in order to compose a painting with a mystical and allegorical essence. "Close your bodily eye so as to perceive your painting first with your mind's eye," he emphasised in 1830, in *Reflections on a Collection of Paintings*. "Then bring to light that which you perceived in the darkness, so that your vision has an influence on others, from the outside in. Painters practise inventing and composing so to speak, but does that mean to say, in other words, that they must assemble and piece things together?" From different origins, the Bavarian Carl Spitzweg devoted himself to caricature and miniature paintings. He understood but moved away from the ambition of his elder, undoubtedly less religious. Why else place cabbages in the foreground?

TURNER, CONSTABLE, BONINGTON

Joseph Mallord William Turner, *Landscape with River and Distant Bay*, England, circa 1835-1840. Oil on canvas, 93 x 123 cm.

I can see nothing or hardly anything of the image. This type of remark may well have been made in front of the large close-ups of skies and swirling matter created by the three English masters. Moreover, such was the discerning reaction of an onlooker in 1814, in front of one of Turner's canvases, admiring his "portraits of nothingness, but extremely true to life". When the reddening brushstroke, rubbed or scraped with a knife, devours three-quarters of the landscape and obliterates the subject, some of the painting still remains to be seen.

John Constable, *Weymouth Bay As the Storm Approaches*, England, circa 1819-1827. Oil on canvas, 88 x 112 cm.

Richard Parkes Bonington, *View of the Normandy Coast*, France, 1823. Oil on canvas, 46.5 x 38.5 cm.

COROT'S FIGURES

They put on an Italian dress and a gypsy coat, they leaf through a book and hold a mandolin, they smooth their hair and dream that they are literary heroines, priestesses, or oriental slaves on a background of undergrowth and fanciful horizons. Corot's figures are professional models - Emma Dobigny for example - or young girls who, when arriving at the studio, reveal the tilt of a head, a twisted posture, or a crumpled blouse. After a few sittings, they sometimes don costumes and an operatic aria, such as *Haydée*, taken straight from the opera by Daniel François Esprit Auber.

Camille Corot, *Haydée*,
Paris, circa 1870-1872.
Oil on canvas, 60 x 44 cm.

Camille Corot, *Portrait of the Artist*, Paris, circa 1825.
Oil on paper glued onto canvas, 32.5 x 24.5 cm.

Camille Corot, *Velléda*,
Paris, circa 1868-1870.
Oil on canvas, 83.5 x 55.5 cm.

Camille Corot, *Young Girl at Her Toilet*, Paris, circa 1860-1865. Oil on cardboard, 34 x 24 cm.

COROT'S LANDSCAPES

Camille Corot, *Memory of Mortefontaine*, France, 1864. Oil on canvas, 65 x 89 cm.

There was a fierce debate between the accomplished and the finished, the highly painted and the excessively loose. At the *Salon* of 1845, Baudelaire took a stand, because "with regard to this so-called clumsiness of Monsieur Corot, it would appear that one might find a small amount of prejudice. - All the semi-intellectuals, after having conscientiously admired one of Corot's paintings, and loyally having given him the praise due, now consider that it has broken the rules in its execution, and all agree that Monsieur Corot positively does not know how to paint. - These good souls, who do not realise […] that there is a great difference between an *accomplished* piece and a *finished* piece - that, in general, that which is *accomplished* is not *finished*, and something that is highly *finished* may not be *accomplished* at all".

Camille Corot, *The Bridge of Mantes*,
Mantes, circa 1868-1870.
Oil on canvas, 38.5 x 55.5 cm.

Camille Corot, *Florence. View from the Boboli Gardens*, Italy, circa 1835-1840. Oil on canvas, 51 x 73.5 cm.

Camille Corot, *Tivoli. The Gardens of the Villa d'Este*, Italy, 1843. Oil on canvas, 43.5 x 60.5 cm.

Théodore Rousseau,
*Group of Oak Trees, Apremont
(Forest of Fontainebleau)*,
Fontainebleau, 1852.
Oil on canvas, 63.5 x 99.5 cm.

Paul Huet,
*Flooding at Saint-Cloud
(Parc de Saint-Cloud)*,
Saint-Cloud, 1855.
Oil on canvas, 203 x 300 cm.

Charles François Daubigny,
The Barges, Île-de-France,
1865. Oil on wood,
38 x 67 cm.

Jean-François Millet, *The Washerwoman*, Barbizon,
circa 1853-1854. Oil on wood, 44 x 33 cm.

Jean-François Millet, *A Winnower*, Barbizon, circa 1848.
Oil on wood, 79.5 x 58.5 cm.

Sketching his subject by the water's edge, in the countryside or at the
house of a countryman, completing a landscape in his Parisian studio in
the northern light and working from memory, or executing the entire
work in the open air, movements of the air and reflections, taking his
canvas and brushes with him... 19th-century artists decided to have the
choice, gradually gaining freedom with regard to an established genre:
the historical or pastoral composed landscape. The motif is close to Paris,
at Saint-Cloud, in the forest of Fontainebleau, or in the hamlet of Barbizon.

A WINDOW, AN EASEL, AND PAINTBOXES:
THE ARTIST'S WORKSHOP

"[…] the novice remained under the spell that captivates born painters at their very first glimpse of a studio in which a few of the material processes of art are revealed. An open window in the archway gave light to the studio of Master Porbus. Concentrated on a canvas hanging from the easel, which still only bore the marks of three or four white lines, the daylight had not yet reached the darkest depths in the corners of that vast room […]. The shelves and consoles were strewn with anatomical models made of plaster, fragments and torsos of ancient goddesses lovingly polished by centuries of caressing".

Honoré de Balzac,
The Unknown Masterpiece, 1831.

△ Léon Cochereau,
Interior of David's Studio,
at the *Collège
des Quatre Nations*, Paris,
1814. Oil on canvas,
90 x 105 cm.

◁ Camille Corot,
Corot's Studio,
Paris, circa 1865-1868.
Oil on canvas, 63 x 42 cm.

△ Painter in
Théodore Géricault's circle,
Young Artist in His Studio,
Paris, circa 1818.
Oil on canvas, 147 x 114 cm.

⊲Left:
Alexandre Gabriel Decamps,
The Painting Monkey, Paris, 1833.
Oil on canvas, 32 x 40 cm.

⊲Right:
Octave Tassaert,
Studio Interior, Paris, 1845.
Oil on canvas, 46 x 38 cm.

△Above:
Achille Michallon, *Study of a Man*,
Paris, pre-1822. Oil on paper
glued onto canvas, 36 x 28.5 cm.

△Above left:
Eugène Delacroix, *Corner
of a Studio. The Stove*,
Paris, circa 1830. Oil on canvas,
51 x 44 cm.

△Above centre:
Eugène Delacroix, *Seated Nude*,
known as Mlle *Rose*,
model from Guérin's studio,
Paris, circa 1820-1823.
Oil on canvas, 81 x 65 cm.

⊲Left:
Christoffer Wilhelm Eckersberg,
The Model, Copenhagen, 1839.
Oil on canvas, 81 x 98 cm.

⊲Right:
Camille Corot, *The Lady in Blue*,
Paris, 1874. Oil on canvas,
80 x 50.5 cm.

BIBLIOGRAPHY

AGHION, Irène, BARBILLON, Claire et LISSARAGUE, François, *Héros et dieux de l'Antiquité. Guide iconographique*, Paris, Flammarion, coll. « Tout l'art/Encyclopédie », 1994.

ARASSE, Daniel, *Le Détail. Pour une histoire rapprochée de la peinture*, Paris, Flammarion, coll. « Champs », 1996.

BALZAC, Honoré DE, *Le Chef-d'œuvre inconnu et autres nouvelles* (1830-1839), éd. Adrien Goetz, Paris, Gallimard, coll. « Folio Classique », 1994.

BANU, Georges, *Le Rideau ou la Fêlure du monde*, Paris, Adam Biro, 1997.

BAUDELAIRE, Charles, *Critique d'art*, suivi de *Critique musicale* (1845-1868), éd. Claude Pichois, Paris, Gallimard, coll. « Folio Essais », 1992.

BAXANDALL, Michael, *L'Œil du Quattrocento*, trad. Yvette Delsaut, Paris, Gallimard, coll. « Bibliothèque illustrée des histoires », 1985.

La Bible de Jérusalem, trad. sous la dir. de l'École biblique de Jérusalem, Paris, Le Cerf, 1988.

CHARPENTIER, Marc Antoine, *La Descente d'Orphée aux enfers* (1686), opéra H. 488 sur un livret anonyme, dir. William Christie, Les Arts florissants, Paris, Erato Disques, 1995.

COLE, Alison, *La Renaissance dans les cours italiennes*, trad. Dennis Collins, Paris, Flammarion, coll. « Tout l'art/Contexte », 1995.

CUZIN, Jean-Pierre, *La Diseuse de bonne aventure de Caravage*, Paris, musée du Louvre, Réunion des musées nationaux, coll. « Les dossiers du département des peintures », 1977.

DAMISCH, Hubert, *L'Origine de la perspective*, Paris, Flammarion, coll. « Champs », 1993.

DELACROIX, Eugène, *Journal. 1822-1863*, éd. Régis Labourdette, préface d'Hubert Damisch, introduction et notes d'André Joubin, Paris, Plon, 1981.

DELAMARE, François et GUINEAU, Bernard, *Les Matériaux de la couleur*, Paris, Gallimard, coll. « Découvertes », 1999.

DESCARTES, René, *Discours de la méthode*, suivi de *La Dioptrique* (1637), Paris, éd. Frédéric de Buzon, Gallimard, coll. « Folio Essais », 1991, et *Œuvres et lettres*, éd. André Bridoux, Paris, Gallimard, coll. « Bibliothèque de la Pléiade », 1937.

DIDEROT, Denis, *Esthétique*, Paris, Laffont, coll. « Bouquins », 1996, vol. 4.

DUCHET-SUCHAUX, Gaston et PASTOUREAU, Michel, *La Bible et les saints. Guide iconographique*, Paris, Flammarion, coll. « Tout l'art/Encyclopédie », nouv. éd. augmentée, 1994.

Encyclopædia Universalis multimédia sur cédérom, France, 1999, version 5.

FARGE, Arlette, *La Vie fragile. Violence, pouvoirs et solidarités à Paris au XVIIIe siècle*, Paris, Le Seuil, coll. « Points Histoire », 1992.

FURETIÈRE, Antoine, *Dictionnaire universel* (1690), rééd. sous la dir. d'Alain Rey, Paris, SNL-Le Robert, 1978, 3 vol.

GAUTIER, Théophile, *Critique d'art : extraits des Salons, 1833-1872*, anthologie composée par M.-H. Girard, Paris, Séguier, coll. « Écrits sur l'art », 1994.

GEORGEL, Pierre et LECOQ, Anne-Marie, *La Peinture dans la peinture*, Paris, Adam Biro, 1987.

GOLDONI, Carlo, *Mémoires : pour servir à l'histoire de sa vie et à celle de son théâtre* (1787), éd. Norbert Jonart, Paris, Aubier, 1992.

GOMBRICH, E.H., *Ombres portées. Leur représentation dans l'art occidental*, trad. Jeanne Bouniort, Paris, Gallimard, coll. « Art et artistes », 1996.

KINTZLER, Catherine, *La France classique et l'opéra ou la Vraisemblance merveilleuse*, Paris, Arles, Harmonia Mundi, 1998, accompagné de 2 disques compacts.

LA FONTAINE, Jean DE, *Contes et nouvelles en vers* (1665-1671), éd. Alain-Marie Bassy, Paris, Gallimard, coll. « Folio Classique », 1982.

LANEYRIE-DAGEN, Nadeije, WAT, Pierre et DAGEN, Philippe, *Le Métier d'artiste. Peintres et sculpteurs depuis le Moyen Âge*, Paris, Larousse, 1999.

LICHTENSCHEIN, Jacqueline (dir.), GROULIER, Jean-François, LANEYRIE-DAGEN, Nadeije et RIOUT, Denys, *La Peinture*, Paris, Larousse, coll. « Textes essentiels », 1995.

MIGNOT, Claude et RABREAU, Daniel (dir.), *Temps modernes. XVe-XVIIIe siècles*, Paris, Flammarion, coll. « Histoire de l'art », 1996.

PROUST, Marcel, *Écrits sur l'art* (1890-1922), éd. Jérôme Picon, Paris, Flammarion, coll. « GF », 1999.

ROLAND MICHEL, Marianne, *Chardin*, Paris, Hazan, 1999.

RONSARD, Pierre DE, *Les Amours* (1552-1556), éd. Henri et Catherine Weber, Paris, Classiques Garnier, 1999.

ROSAND, David, *La Trace de l'artiste. Léonard et Titien*, trad. Jeanne Bouniort, Paris, Gallimard, coll. « Art et artistes », 1993.

ROSENBERG, Pierre (dir.), *Watteau. 1684-1721*, cat. exp., Paris, Galeries nationales du Grand Palais, Réunion des musées nationaux, 1984, en particulier François MOUREAU, « Watteau dans son temps » et « Iconographie théâtrale », pp. 471-508 et 509-528.
Fragonard. 1732-1806, cat. exp., Paris, Galeries nationales du Grand Palais, Réunion des musées nationaux, 1987.
Nicolas Poussin. 1594-1665, cat. exp., Paris, Galeries nationales du Grand Palais, Réunion des musées nationaux, 1994, en particulier Avigdor ARIKHA, « De la boîte, des figurines et du mannequin », pp. 44-47.

ROUSSEAU, Jean-Jacques, *Émile ou De l'éducation* (1762), éd. Charles Wirtz et Pierre Burgelin, Paris, Gallimard, coll. « Folio Essais », 1995.

VAN GOGH, Vincent, *Correspondance générale*, trad. Maurice Beerblock et Louis Roëlandt, Paris, Gallimard, coll. « Biblos », 1990, 3 vol.

VOVELLE, Michel (dir.), *L'Homme des Lumières*, Paris, Le Seuil, coll. « L'univers historique », 1996, en particulier Daniel ARASSE, « L'artiste », pp. 253-284.

WESTERMANN, Mariët, *Le Siècle d'or en Hollande*, trad. Isabelle Leymarie, Paris, Flammarion, coll. « Tout l'art/Contexte », 1996.

WITTKOWER, Rudolf et Margot, *Les Enfants de Saturne. Psychologie et comportement des artistes de l'Antiquité à la Révolution française*, trad. Daniel Arasse, Paris, Macula, 1991.

INDEX OF ARTISTS

CRÉDITS PHOTOGRAPHIQUES

RMN : Arnaudet ; Bellot ; Berizzi ; Bernard ; Blot ;
Chenot ; Chuzeville ; Coursaget ; Jean ; Lewandowski ;
Marbœuf ; Néri ; Ojeda ; Raux ; Schormans.

PHOTOGRAVURE : Arciel Graphic

Achevé d'imprimer
le 20 juillet 2002
par Les Presses de Bretagne, Rennes

Dépôt légal : Août 2002